THE TORNADO

THE TORNADO

John Edward Weems

Doubleday & Company, Inc., Garden City, New York
1977

Library of Congress Cataloging in Publication Data

Weems, John Edward.
The Tornado.

Includes bibliographical references and index.
ISBN: 0-385-07178-7
Library of Congress Catalog Card Number 76–44055

To the memory of the 114 individuals
who lost their lives in The Tornado.
Their names appear in the
Acknowledgments and Bibliography section.

And to the memory of my father and mother,
J. Eddie Weems, Sr.,
November 13, 1896–July 11, 1976.
Anna Lee Scott Weems,
June 22, 1901–July 11, 1976.

Contents

ILLUSTRATIONS
Plates following page 84

Cirrus clouds
Mammatocumulus
Squall line clouds
Distant thunderstorm
Developing funnel
Tornado
1919 Nebraska tornado
1884 South Dakota tornado
Waco damage
Franklin Avenue, Waco
City, county map showing damage area
Cleaning up wreckage
Days later
Austin Avenue today, the Mall
Brazos River, city in the distance
The *Brazos Queen*
Author, father, ranch windmill, 1976

(See the Acknowledgments and Bibliography section for picture credits.)

THE TORNADO

1

THE CLOUD

Extended drought had left plant life brittle brown, as if from a hard freeze. Deep cracks cut through depleted soil: chapped lips of earth waiting for relief that could come only from plentiful moisture.

Stunted buffalo grass lining the banks of an empty, stony creek retained the prints of a man's shoes long after he had walked across it. The parched vegetation had lost its green resilience. On rocky hills nearby, where sun glare compounded searing heat, grass tufts disintegrated underfoot and mixed with sandy soil.

I was with my father on his 320-acre Texas ranch, helping him provide water for thirsty cattle. The rock-bottomed creek that usually trickled into late-summer months before drying up completely afforded no help now, even though the date was only May 11. An auxiliary water supply, a windmill, stood waiting near the same creek, but the windmill had been given such hard use in recent months that the deep, spring-fed well from which it drew water was running perilously low.

More immediately unpleasant for us was the knowledge that something had gone wrong with the reciprocating vertical rod used to transmit power from wind-driven wheel above to pump below, so that the mechanism would not work properly. To get water for bony cattle now hiding from raw sunshine in dust-powdered thickets somewhere around us, we had to disconnect the vertical rod at a location about two feet above the pump, then do the wind's job with gloved hands. Working single stints for as long as we were able, we would bend over the now-shortened rod and force down-and-up motions on it, quickly exhausting ourselves. The hard work caused water to spill from a pipe into a huge, circular concrete trough in a stream that impressed us as being very small for all the agony that went into the chore.

The labor required frequent breathing spells. One of us would pause from his work for a rest, sweating and burning under the midday sun, while the other would take over until he had used up, for the moment, his own arms, shoulders, back, and lungs. Despite this torture, there came occasional relief from the stinging sunshine when a lone cumulus cloud would place itself between us and our fiery persecutor long enough to cast a delicious shadow and make us wish for more.

So there *was* enough moisture somewhere to form clouds, even if we weren't getting our share of the 1,500 cubic miles of water said to fall on the United States annually—enough to cover the land to a depth of two and a half feet if it ever should come in a single deluge. During recent weeks, with the wind often blowing hot and dry from the west, the sky usually had been devoid even of those lofty powder puffs. Frequently they signify nothing more than dry weather ahead unless, as occurs sometimes in summer mugginess, they silently sail off to some rendezvous, pile up into a high-reaching cloud blossom known as cumulonimbus (a thunderhead), and make their way back. Whenever that happens, those once-puny puffs can truly assert themselves, by rocking the countryside with sounds of a cannonade and by spearing the landscape with forks of lightning.

No wonder thunderstorms have figured prominently in legends and myths! Their awesomeness surely inspired reverential fear in the first human beings who observed their alarming displays. But at an early date human intelligence also would have admitted their value. Two beliefs prevalent among North American Indians attest to this.

Pueblo Indians believed their deceased tribesmen became clouds and returned to them with rain. Apaches looked upon the lightning and thunder of mighty rainstorms as capable of giving power to themselves and fellow tribesmen. Although those Apaches logically considered severe thunderstorms to have been evilly inspired, they recognized the goodness and the necessity of mild storms. The lightning they considered to be the arrow of Thunder People; its flash was the arrow's flight. The ensuing roar supposedly came from a real person responsible for sending all that tumult.

About the only sounds and sights we were aware of that day on the ranch, however, were rhythmical gurgles coming from somewhere deep in the pump and an ensuing thin but continual swish of water as we added fractions of inches to the trough level.

Further, we held out little hope for the future of those white fluffs scudding overhead. Their lives would be brief, we guessed. The cumulus had been born when rising warm air entered a cooler level above the earth. At that point, condensation had occurred. The small water droplets thus formed had given the clouds their cottony shapes seen by observers far below. But these cumulus, all floating in from the southeast, surely would disappear later on. That much and a little more I knew, or thought I knew, about clouds, having stumbled through a navy course in meteorology years earlier.

During one rest halt, I stood dripping sweat in the midst of that excruciating drought and reflected for a few minutes more on the weather, especially on its vagaries. At that very moment, other Americans were up to their waists in water. Low areas of one town little more than two hundred miles southeast of us had been flooded recently by thunderstorms. People there would

have been delighted to change places with us. Better to have too
little water, they surely would have said, than to have it come
slithering under a door like a snake, eventually covering carpets,
furniture, and maybe even roof. On the other hand, any cattle
those people owned wouldn't have been very thirsty, if any had
survived drowning.

The weather is nature's way of imparting badly needed humil-
ity to men and women, I reflected. Some men of great creative
intelligence had devised a way to travel above those scattered
cumulus floating far overhead. Others had discovered how to
transmit pictures through the very atmosphere that seemed almost to suffocate us—pictures that could be seen provided one
owned intricate electronic equipment manufactured for the purpose. A number of masterminds had been able to build a bomb
that could kill people by the hundreds of thousands. Other men
of brilliance had devoted themselves to building rockets and mis-
siles for carrying such destruction farther and faster.

Not one of those geniuses, however, could tell the world how
to turn off a rainstorm before too much water fell. Not one of
them could have procured water at that moment in any manner
other than the primitive, back-breaking method we were using.
Any scientific rainmaker would have had to wait for the appearance of a natural cloud already pregnant with rain before seeding it with ice crystals or silver iodide—and even then he could
never know exactly how much of the ensuing shower might have
been his responsibility and how much of it had been nature's.

So the weather can humble any man. It can even make some
of those awesome inventions of his seem puny. A rainstorm of
moderate intensity releases energy at the rate of three old-style
atomic bombs every second. To equal the kinetic energy of one
hurricane of moderate size it would be necessary to explode a
thousand atomic bombs a minute. Humbling indeed! But
weather can prove absolutely humiliating, I reflected further, to
men whose desperation would allow them to take as many as
three years off their lives by pumping water for parched cattle
on a miserably hot day like this.

Ironically, it was to have been my day off from work as telegraph editor of a daily newspaper nearby. I certainly had made other plans, but the weather remained master of men. It was my turn at the pump.

Among the many things I *didn't* know about our weather that Monday, May 11, was that nature was on the verge of sending us its idea of bountiful help. Had we possessed the newest radar-scope and weather maps, plus a capacity for interpreting them correctly, we might have foreseen this. But we didn't have so much as a workable windmill, one of man's simpler technological inventions and a piece of machinery that even I could under-stand, if not repair.

Weather maps for that day and several preceding ones had carried little messages of hope for owners of land and cattle shriveling in the Southwest, although we were unaware of this at the time. Apparently some local forecasters ignored the signs, too.

Four days earlier, on May 7, a great mass of cold air had begun invading the United States from the Pacific, many hun-dreds of miles to the northwest of us, along the coasts of Wash-ington, Oregon, and northern California. The cold front had con-tinued to creep in behind a low-pressure system, so that on the following day it appeared (on a weather map I examined later) to be oriented north-south, from Montana to Arizona. This was still to the west of us. A line marking its location was spotted at intervals with small arrows pointing in our general direction. They might have been pins marking unit locations of a mighty army racing to save us from more insufferable heat, since weather generally moves from west to east in the middle lati-tudes.

Far to the northeast of us on that same map appeared a high-pressure system dominating the eastern half of the United States, and thus no doubt out of our way. Good! We didn't want that— not the fair, hot days that cells of high pressure usually mean in our part of the country during late spring, summer, and early au-tumn. Instead we yearned for the change brought by lows: clouds and wind.

Still, that eastern high-pressure system was affecting us.* For reasons that I learned in meteorology class but wouldn't care to repeat in exhaustive detail here, even if I could remember them, Northern Hemisphere air flows clockwise and outward around a high-pressure cell (counterclockwise and inward around a low). This happened to mean for us that the eastern high was sending winds circling outward from its center for hundreds of miles: over several southeastern states, across the tepid Gulf of Mexico, and back into our own baked area. I was unaware that day of the presence of much breeze or atmospheric moisture, but they must have been there. The weather map I examined later indicated this.

Had I known at the time what the meteorologist who prepared that map must have known or suspected, I'd have gone home to get raincoat, hood, and rubber boots instead of waiting around that windmill to pump water like a mindless robot. Whenever great masses of cold, dry air and warm, moist air collide, "bad" weather results—"bad," anyway, in the words of those golden throats who give forecasts on radio and television several times daily without having any idea about the level of their own city water supply. Resulting "bad" weather can mean rain, at best. At worst, it might also mean storm winds and hail.

For corroboration I refer to an issue of the *Monthly Weather Review* that appeared not long after Miserable Monday, the day we pumped water on the ranch. Although the article obviously wasn't written for the simple understanding of any former student of a single course in meteorology, the author included—and possibly not for his readers, either—it can be comprehended. Substitute "low pressure" for "trough" and "high pressure" for "ridge," remember "counterclockwise winds" around a low and "clockwise winds" around a high, and keep a dictionary handy for the rest. Then we can all see the significance posed for Southwesterners by the weather features of that May 11.

> . . . [The] circulation over the United States was domi-
> nated by a trough in the West and a ridge in the East,
> both of which had height departures from normal of

---

* Such a system is sometimes called an anticyclone, as opposed to a cyclone, or low-pressure system.

about equal magnitude (−12 over Nevada, +11 over South Carolina). This circulation provided a stronger-than-normal flow of air from the Gulf of Mexico northward through the central part of the country, and also an abnormally strong eastward flux of cool Pacific air through the Southwest trough into the region east of the Rockies. . . . It is believed that a large-scale circulation pattern of this type is especially favorable for the development of severe squall lines and tornadic activity since it provides for more frequent and more intense interactions between the maritime polar and maritime tropical air masses than would normally occur. It has long been recognized, of course, that intense squall lines and tornadoes are most favored synoptically where cold, dry Pacific air masses are advected rapidly aloft over moist tropical air in lower levels.

Squall lines and other turbulence, however, seemed far removed from us that dry day. Even a few golden throats in our vicinity had peered around outside the shelter of their radio and television studios and had realized the need for rain. They were beginning to express hopes accordingly. But, as the eleventh day of the fifth month dawned and progressed, they, and we, had little more than hope to go on. The meteorologist who produced that weather map I studied later apparently resided in another part of the country and was not forecasting for us, or else he prepared the map afterward with the benefit of vast hindsight. The prediction as carried that day in our local newspaper, the one for which I worked, had said only, "Partly cloudy today and Tuesday; a few thunderstorms along the [Gulf] coast."

Nearly two hundred miles separated us from the coast and those spotty thunderstorms; so on May 11 we were hoping for little more than a favorable forecast at some future date.

The cumulus clouds multiplied even as we worked the pump. This gave me an opportunity to pontificate on the origin of their name. My father, who had become a captive audience the moment he asked me to help with the watering, listened.

Once again I relied on meteorological knowledge acquired in

a few months of study completed ten years earlier at the Navy V-12 unit of Carson-Newman College, Jefferson City, Tennessee. The Latin word for "heap" gave us the cloud designation "cumulus," and it was appropriate. Those vapory vessels floating across the skies looked more like heaps of cotton piled on invisible carriers than anything else. The same Latin word also gave us the term "accumulate." I injected this into the conversation, too, before it became my turn to pump again.

Our physical reserve, especially mine, was waning quickly now, but the water level in the trough had reached respectable depth. Still, if an Indian rain dance could have assured a shower, I would have been willing to perform one in breechcloth at the nearest crowded street intersection. Such reflection jostled my thoughts back to the helplessness of mankind when pitted against the weather. Probably since man and woman faced their first adversity from the atmosphere, they had been striving to do something about it. I recalled reading about primitive people sacrificing animals and even other human beings to gods who caused too much or too little rain, and about other tribes who threw spears toward an approaching storm to kill the spirit that was directing its movement.

More recently I have read about some other peculiar beliefs—these in regard to various peoples who believed they could control the winds. Along the Lena River Basin in Siberia, a region best known for its chilling temperatures during much of the year,† there lived a people called Yakuts, to whom warm weather proved uncomfortable. If a Yakut happened to be making a lengthy journey during a hot spell he took a stone that he chanced to find in an animal or fish, wound a horsehair around it several times, and tied it to a stick. Then he waved the stick about, uttering an incantation. After that he waited and waited, and when a cool breeze sprang up the pleased Yakut assumed he had been responsible. If he wanted an extended cool breeze— one of up to nine days—he commenced the sorcery by dipping his holy stone into the blood of a bird or a beast. Then he presented the little red-dripping rock to the sun and completed

† But Siberia can get hot, too. Temperatures range from almost 100 degrees below zero to more than 100 above.

some more magical hoopla before settling down to await comfortable traveling conditions.

To repeat, I have only read about that strange practice. I never have visited the Lena River Basin to verify it firsthand and am not likely to do so, considering the number of people reportedly being detained in Siberia despite their wish to leave. Further, this sorcery was described by two European travelers who visited the area and wrote about it long ago, in the mid-eighteenth and the mid-nineteenth centuries. Possibly the Yakuts no longer believe they can create a cool breeze. On the other hand, they might have blown themselves away seeking to escape the heat of ensuing summers. But I doubt that. I think they still inhabit the basin of the Lena River, and many of them probably live there in ignorance of televised weather forecasts.

Those Yakuts, however, weren't singular—just odd. Other human beings have had hopes as grandiose as they in regard to ruling the elements. In southern Africa, a Hottentot used to believe he could stop a high wind by unfurling an animal skin on the end of a pole and forcing the breeze to gust itself out against that fluttering barrier. In North America, an Omaha Indian flapped his blanket to raise a wind that would drive away mosquitoes. But if his success in getting rid of those pests was on the same level as mine he was well named. "Omaha" means (according to my Webster's) "going upstream or against the wind."

Off Cape York, Australia, in the Torres Strait, natives of Murray Island summoned a strong southeasterly wind by arranging coconut leaves and other vegetation to point toward two specified granite boulders near the shore. They had the practical sense to do this only during the season of the southeast monsoon, and not during another time of year known in their part of the world as the northwest monsoon.

In Finland, wizards once manufactured wind for sale to desirous mariners. They delivered their goods in a length of rope tied with three knots. When a seaman untied the first knot he felt a moderate wind soon afterward. When he loosened the second knot he got a half gale. When, or if, he undid the third knot he immediately faced the blast of a full hurricane. Exactly why anyone would sell a hurricane to a poor sailor isn't explained in any reference book I have searched, but the seaman surely must have untied the third one only in sheer desperation, after loosening the first two and finding malfunctions.

The Finns seem to have outgrown that belief in the prowess of their wizards, but some peasant neighbors to the south, across the Gulf of Finland, in Estonia, are said still to blame Finnish sorcerers for the bitter northerly winds that perennially sweep across their countryside every spring, bringing with them the agonies of ague and rheumatism. Estonian peasants even celebrate their blind belief with a bit of oft-sung folk music:

> Wind of the Cross! rushing and mighty!
> Heavy the blow of thy wings sweeping past!
> Wild wailing wind of misfortune and sorrow,
> Wizards of Finland ride by on the blast.

Those lines have had a great impact on me since the first time I read them. Having just examined them again, I can almost believe in that silly superstition myself. But if the effect on others is lessened by the vast differences separating our world from such a faraway place, I might mention that an American author, Richard Henry Dana, himself contributed to perpetuating the legend in *Two Years Before the Mast*. It is said, Dana wrote, that seamen beating against the wind in the Gulf of Finland sometimes sight a sail far astern. Quickly the strange ship overhauls them, slicing through churning seas under swollen sails and straining ropes. The awed sailors know then that the mystery ship hails from Finland, where people seem to own the wind.

Corroboration comes more easily in other areas. Humanity *has* established some control over weather, as shown by irrigation systems centuries old; paved roads and tall bridges; smudge pots holding off freezes in California, Florida, and Texas orchards; airport devices enabling planes to take off and land despite widespread fog; sports arenas with vast roofs keeping out rain and wind as well as sunshine; buildings and even covered shopping malls with temperatures centrally regulated the year around.

Beyond that, human beings have created small tornadoes, in science laboratories and in a few war-scarred cities, where ascending heat from bombs and fires proved sufficient for the formation of miniature "twisters" when the heat met colder air above. Tornadoes also have been formed by hot air rising from forest fires. Many years ago, Apache Indians became aware of the reasons behind this phenomenon and put it to their own use. Those remarkable observers would create for desert signaling their own "dust devils" (they might be called small tornadoes), using the artificial heat of blazing cactus plants to start a whirling updraft.

Some contemporary scientists have tinkered with hurricanes— and apparently with limited success at reducing the heat energy and the mighty winds they believe are driven by that heat. They have done this by seeding selected storm clouds that were still far at sea, so that supercooled droplets of water were frozen immediately, thus releasing heat that otherwise might have gone into a more dangerous generation of hurricane fury. Tests conducted on the spot by airplanes seemed to prove that the seeding resulted in some decrease of wind velocity. These scientists hope that if release of heat energy can be made to take place over a large area while the hurricane is still at sea, the violence of its winds might be lessened before the storm strikes land.

Speculations by certain other weather wizards in the early days of the atomic bomb suggested that a hurricane could possibly be broken up while still at sea by exploding in its midst one of those superbombs, which strikes me as having little more logic than ridding the Far West of earthquakes by blowing up California. Further, in view of the strength of hurricanes as compared with atomic bombs, it seems unlikely that only one explosion would do the job. In any event, with such expansive thinkers as those on the loose, civilization might be less in need of additional scientific progress than of regulatory bodies to assure meteorological moderation—like the Connecticut Weather Control Board, which was optimistically "set up in the 1960s during a drought [according to its 1975 chairman, state Agriculture Commissioner George Wilber] to control rain-producing functions and make sure people didn't hurt anybody with rain dances and cloud-seeding and that sort of thing."

Had I read that statement before the dry day on my father's

ranch I should have thought it rather more facetious than it was. Still, I realize that the human race has reached such a level of intelligence that it can do itself and this planet great harm as well as good. Although we obviously can't control the weather to our complete benefit, we can and do exert some influence, which is more likely to be harmful than helpful—a fact that says something else about mankind's intelligence level. Men have changed entire climates by replacing vast forests with pastures and farms, according to numerous observers, including H. G. Wells (in *The Outline of History*). Those results have shown that nature knew more than mankind about how best to function.

More recently, another author, Ruth Kirk (in *Desert: the American Southwest*), penned a vivid description of a change of similar misfortune that came to Arizona. When "manifest destiny" sent Americans pressing westward, a belief popular among them was that an absence of agriculture caused the aridity there. As soon as "green fields and grazing animals" covered the land, more rain would fall, they thought.

Instead, "grazing left the soil vulnerable to erosion. Wind caught sand and drifted it, smothering what grass cover remained. Runoff churned and rushed like torrents of liquid sandpaper, and cloudburst after cloudburst intensified the process."

Other parts of the world have suffered in a similar manner. Expanding human and livestock populations, combined with climatological changes that encourage desert encroachment, have become a major problem in Africa, Asia, and Latin America, according to Erik Eckholm of Worldwatch Institute. Good land there has been ruined by erosion, increased flooding, and a loss of fertility. As a result, he said (in a paper presented to the 142nd annual meeting of the American Association for the Advancement of Science), "Marginal people on marginal lands will slowly sink into the slough of hopeless poverty." This probably will also bring on international problems and conflicts for governments to resolve.

Some scientists foresee the same infertility for the American Great Plains, and for the same reasons. Henry Lansford of the National Center for Atmospheric Research wrote in a recent issue of *Smithsonian* magazine, "The climate trends that some scientists are predicting could bring us to a point of catastrophic convergence between the increasing population and inadequate food supplies much sooner than many people expect."

Other noticeable climatological change has resulted from the construction of metropolitan skyscrapers, which have altered rainfall patterns in their immediate vicinity. Dr. Joseph L. Goldman, associate director of the Institute for Storm Research at the University of Saint Thomas in Houston, has examined the effect of tall buildings in his area and has discovered "[they] act as a mountain to the wind. . . . We now find that it is drier in the downtown area where it used to be wet before. The west used to be dry relative to the downtown area and the east [because the west is farther from the primary source of moisture, the Gulf of Mexico]."

Dr. Goldman explained the specific reason for this. Those tall buildings throw upward moist southeasterly wind currents blowing from the Gulf, causing clouds to form. Rain then falls downwind from (or westward of) the Houston skyscrapers.

Changes in rainfall patterns probably can be seen in other large cities around the world, he believes.

Some scientists have attributed to mankind a different effect upon the weather, a truly ominous one. Among these authorities is Dr. Reid Bryson of the University of Wisconsin Institute for Environmental Studies. Dr. Bryson said recently that until the present century only giant volcanic eruptions could pour huge amounts of dust and other particles into the atmosphere.‡ Now "man himself is quite a volcano." Current activities result in vomiting into the air 408 million metric tons of particles annually from industry, waste disposal, and transportation, and from hydrocarbons, nitrates, and converted sulfates.

Until half a century ago mankind's influence on climate had been slight, Dr. Bryson elaborated. But with the advent earlier of the Industrial Revolution (which eventually brought an

‡ A tremendous eruption in 1815 of an Indonesian volcano named Tambora is said by some scientists to have been responsible for America's "summerless" year of 1816 by flooding the atmosphere with volcanic ash and reducing the sun's warming effect. That year, a snowstorm swept northeastern states on June 6. July and August were almost as chilly.

atmospheric carbon dioxide increase of an estimated 10 per cent), and especially during the past fifty years, "[man's influence on the climate] is quite comparable to natural causes."

In view of ice ages and other momentous developments, some climatologists will disagree with this broad statement, but no one can ignore mankind's recently realized capacity for causing a few weather changes. Exactly how the climate might be altered if people continue their current atmospheric pollution is still debatable, but one thing seems assured. We can only suffer as a result of recent indiscretions.

Considering the human inventive capacity, then, maybe it isn't so ridiculous that another function of the Connecticut Weather Control Board is said (by another member, meteorologist Paul Waggoner) to be to discuss and examine such activities as artificially suppressing lightning and hail, and using fire to dissipate airport fog. I'm certainly not knowledgeable enough to declare that there never will be a place for the board in future Connecticut administrations, even though Chairman Wilber did say (no doubt with a smile) that the last scheduled meeting "was called off because of rain."

Potential danger from man-created weather has influenced even treaty makers. At a 1975 disarmament discussion in Geneva, American and Russian negotiators proposed a treaty banning hostile use of the man-made changes of nature. They were looking to the future—a bit of foresight that might save much sorrow if more of us would follow suit.

"I don't think we have any way [now] of creating a tidal wave . . . or . . . [any] idea how to form . . . or steer a hurricane," said the chief negotiator for the United States, Joseph Martin, Jr. "[But] fifty years ago you talked about breaking the atom and [about] laser guns, and it was all taken as Buck Rogers. Now these things are with us. . . . The trouble is you cannot predict what man can invent."

Martin might have added that once man has created a monster he can't disinvent it. The poor Estonian peasants who have been plagued for years by those Finnish wind wizards would have supported him.

Martin's remarks weren't on my mind that day at the ranch. I read them later, along with several other observations mentioned here. But the subject of man and weather certainly was on my mind then.

I finished what proved to be my last turn at the pump, looked at the water level in that trough, and reflected silently that if men can't control the weather, at least two weak mortals had created a circular pond of cool water in the heart of a drought-stricken land, all in a matter of an hour or so.

Until this time, we had refrained from making any noise that might have been construed by distant cattle as being calls to come quench their thirst, so that we might avoid annihilation under the crush of numerous hoofs. Now, with the huge trough full, we felt safe in summoning them. We commenced shouting the only word our animals understood: "S-s-w-w-o-o-o-o! S-s-w-w-o-o-o-o!"

Then we saw them coming, a few at first, from out of those distant, dusty thickets where they had sought shelter from the blazing sun. They didn't run—these cattle, like most others, rarely ran unless frightened—but they certainly did hurry, relieved to know that we intended to sustain their lives for at least one more day.

We stood well back and listened while the first three or four animals drank. Heads lowered into the trough, they took in water with swirling noises rather like the way children are taught never to eat soup, only more so. Not all the cattle had answered our summons, however, and we faced the task of walking through and around thickets to bring them in. For half an hour or more we searched several wooded areas on the ranch, which my father proudly describes as remaining mostly the same as it was a hundred, even a thousand, years ago.* Never has it been cultivated, to his knowledge. Never have trees been chopped down without good reason; never have pesticides been used there. He won't even allow the shooting of wild fowl or animals on the place. Consequently, although his land then comprised

---

* Sadly I must add a qualification here and for later consideration in the text, although I feel the present tense should stand. My father and mother died in an automobile accident (for which they were blameless) on July 11, 1976.

only 320 acres (considered a large ranch in dudish California, maybe, but not in many other states), a wanderer could lose himself in densely forested parts of it.

I remember standing that day in one wooded area looking for hidden cattle when I happened to glance skyward, toward the highest branches of several towering old pecan trees that grew near the creek. Beyond them and their warm background of blue I noticed to westward the anvil-like top of a giant thunderstorm cloud that had crept up on us while we were engaged in activities other than weather watching and denunciation. If any rumbles of distant thunder had reached us, we must have attributed them subconsciously to the firing of big guns at an army post in our vicinity.

Later, peering at the cloud from a clearing, I saw an awesome example of cumulonimbus. Its long, flat, dark base seemed to merge with the distant horizon. Atop the base were stacked what I took to be those cumulus clouds we had seen scudding overhead earlier in the day. Now united, they looked like monumental cotton bolls piled heavenward, except at the very peak. There, at an altitude of as much as 75,000 feet—more than fourteen miles above the earth—winds had blown the highest clouds into the shape of a flat-topped crown for this meteorological majesty.

2

COMING CLOSER

Our satisfaction increased as the western horizon darkened. Although we couldn't yet be certain of receiving so much as a sprinkle of relief, this weather obviously was moving from west to east, as it should be doing to corroborate some old proverbs. One was, "Eastward the course of the weather makes its way," apparently borrowing some words, but not direction, from that adage about empires.

For thousands of years people have been putting their weather observations into proverbs, and, considering our own limited experience that day with the miseries of present conditions and the nagging uncertainties about future developments, I could understand why. Living with an unknown and unpredictable tomorrow would have become unendurable to the first men and women, especially when weather governed their existence to the extent that it did then. A bit of silliness described its grip:

What is it molds the life of man?
    The weather.
What makes some black and others tan?
    The weather.
What makes the Zulu live in trees,
And Congo natives dress in leaves,
While others go in furs and freeze?
    The weather.

Eskimos don't "go in furs and freeze." They might dress in furs, but they live in harmony with nature (like other primitive peoples of any time and place), and thus they usually live in reasonable comfort, as explorer Vilhjalmur Stefansson wrote in *The Friendly Arctic*. Still, the verse makes its point: weather has owned mankind at least into the twentieth century, and it possesses him today in ways he might not realize.

Several scientists, including Dr. Helmut E. Landsberg of the University of Maryland (and former director of climatology with the U. S. Weather Bureau), recently discussed these ways. Among arthritic patients a falling barometer, which affects fluid-filled cavities in body joints, and rising humidity will cause greater pain. People suffering from respiratory ailments will find breathing more difficult during a period of air stagnation, when a lack of wind can result in atmospheric pollution. Individuals subject to unusual mood changes might find dark, overcast days exceptionally depressing and the long nights common to parts of the globe impossible to endure. For some persons a period of hot, humid weather can ignite violence or suicide. Sunshiny days encourage migraine headache attacks. Temperature fluctuations —not extended low temperature—bring on the common cold (certain British researchers have found), probably because of an ensuing strain on the heat-regulator system of the human body that results in chilling and in weakening resistance to germs. Warm weather causes a drop in blood pressures of persons with hypertension; cold results in an increase.

These are some of the physiological reactions to weather. We all know the more obvious ways in which weather holds sway over mankind—for instance, in the winter, when shoveling snow results in heart attacks and hazardous driving conditions cause fatalities. The National Weather Service has kept records of such deaths. It has found that from 1936 to 1969 winter storms killed more than three thousand Americans. Fewer than four hundred deaths, however, were a direct result of exposure. The rest came in automobile accidents (one third of the total) and in other indirect ways.

"What is it molds the life of man? The weather." It has done so, and it still does. We can all appreciate the reason for anxieties among the earliest human beings about what tomorrow might bring. Fishermen a thousand years removed from today's tuna and shrimp fleets and their access to scientific forecasts needed to know whether they would be sailing on a clear, calm Monday into a stormy Tuesday or Wednesday. Centuries ago, farmers, too, benefited in several obvious ways by having advance notice about the arrival of rain. Any of our remotest ancestors gained by being warned of impending weather changes. Thus the wisest and probably longest-lived of them became sagacious observers.

Their rules for foretelling various changes eventually went into proverbs. Some early examples have been found on Babylonian clay tablets dating back to 4000 B.C. A number of proverbs are applicable even today, anywhere in the world. They were originated by sky watchers who had successfully determined the actual order of weather phenomena, although they couldn't even guess at causes. Other weather sayings have proved valid only for the particular localities where they were formulated: areas in valleys or near mountains or water that influenced weather conditions in the immediate vicinity and rendered proverbs from those places misleading or meaningless for the rest of the world. Finally, a number of maxims based on superstition, fancy, or ignorance (like the story of the groundhog and its shadow) are known now as totally false.

Many of the workable proverbs are remarkable for accuracy established long before the invention, by two Italians, of basic forecasting instruments: the thermometer, developed by Galileo about 1593, and the barometer, invented by Evangelista Torricelli in 1643 and immediately recognized as a momentous device. If the liquid in a barometer fell, observers soon realized, a period of storminess likely followed. If the liquid rose, fair weather could be expected.

Antedating both instruments, however, were these verses from the sixteenth chapter of Matthew.

He answered and said unto them, When it is evening, ye say, It will be fair weather: for the sky is red.
And in the morning, It will be foul weather to day: for the sky is red and lowring.

The same general forecast appears in this ancient jingle:

Sky red in the morning
Is a sailor's sure warning.
Sky red at night
Is the sailor's delight.

The phenomenon first recognized by people ages ago is explainable in a simple way now, although any meteorologist would go into greater detail. In the first place, "morning" and "evening" were referred to because those were the times of day when a modified appearance of the sun was most noticeable, although atmospheric conditions that produced the effects mentioned could occur at any hour. Beyond that, there's this explanation: Rainless days always have been heralded by that "evening red" mentioned, and by "morning gray." A setting sun shining clearly and reddening the western sky gives proof of the absence of clouds for a long distance westward. Since weather usually comes from the west, as we now know, such a red sky at evening would indeed foretell fair weather for a while afterward. If the night is clear and the upper air dry, cooling by radiation will be so favored that it will likely cause water condensation on cold dust particles sufficient to produce a fog and, at dawn, "morning gray."

But let a day or two pass. Suppose the western sky becomes banked with clouds at sunset, giving an "evening gray," or some morning a rising red sun brightens the eastern horizon and colors the underside of a "lowring" cloud sheet. Dry weather then obviously lies to eastward. Clouds becoming heavier and lower, heralding rain, will approach from the west.

Direction of weather movement as known now also explains
the accuracy of another proverb:

> Rainbow in the morning, sailors take warning.
> Rainbow at night, sailor's delight.

A morning sun shining from the east would create a rainbow
on clouds in the west—again, the direction from which showers
and storms usually come. On the other hand, a rainbow formed
by an evening sun shining eastward would color clouds located
beyond threat to the observer.

A notable shortcoming in this ancient morning-evening
method of folk forecasting lay in an inability to do much good
guessing during hours in between: at night, when key conditions
weren't easily discernible, and during the day, when atmospheric
conditions producing such effects as "red and lowring" weren't
conspicuous enough for primitive forecasters who relied upon
the sun's modified appearance for predictions. For their purposes
they needed to examine the sun through a great thickness of air
—that is, when it was near a horizon: at sunrise or sunset.

Some of those old-timers attempted night forecasting, but
without great success. They *did* have imagination, however, as
their beliefs about a "dry moon" and a "wet moon" proved. If the
moon's "horns" tipped upward, the ensuing month would be one
of fair weather, because the moon would be able to hold water
instead of allowing it to cascade down upon the populace. If
those "horns" bent downward, the next few weeks would be
sloppy ones.

As we now know, nothing from that whole theory holds any
water at all. The moon exerts no noticeable, persistent influence
on weather, except for whatever small atmospheric effect tides
might have. Some ancient, disgusted iconoclast, perhaps risking
his neck to correct another popular fallacy, prepared this truthful
weather proverb for dissemination, even though individuals on
the lowest rungs of intelligence might have hissed at his profana-
tion:

> The moon and the weather
> May change together,
> But a change in the moon
> Does not change the weather.

That dry day on the ranch, my father and I would have been willing to accept help in changing current weather conditions from any source: the moon, Finnish wizards, Yakuts, H. G. Wells, the Connecticut Weather Control Board—even the Great Communist Conspiracy, provided they wouldn't flood us. Further glances westward, however, showed us that nature itself seemed indeed to have taken pity. The big cloud had moved a little closer, although it appeared also to be sliding a bit far northward for our complacence. Some people were enjoying drought-breaking downpours for sure, but they were dozens of miles removed from us.

I stood there still dripping sweat from head nearly to toe, and still hoping. Another weather proverb, this one North American Indian, might have applied to me if interpreted broadly. Indians used to say, "When locks turn damp in the scalp house, surely it will rain." My locks were soaked, for certain, but fortunately my scalp was housed where I preferred it to be; so the saying might not have been expected to hold true. Still, those old Indians had logic on their side. The same humidity that dampened all that burgled hair was capable also of bringing showers or downpours —or worse.

Soon we saw that the great cloud had developed a green tinge against a background now almost black. That meant hail, although I can't quote a weather proverb right now to prove it. Undeterred, we continued to hope that the monster would come our way. Into each life some hail must fall, no doubt, but for us shriveled central Texans the rain would make it bearable.

Had we been listening to news broadcasts that afternoon our desires regarding the weather might have been modified, but I doubt it. Unknown to us, about the same time we had been completing the creation of our miniature lake, a state highway patrol car some two hundred miles away to westward had begun following a recently sighted funnel cloud, one of several (as we learned later) born that day in our part of the country.

The car had been patrolling a section of U. S. Highway 87 forty or fifty miles northwest of San Angelo, Texas, when its two occupants sighted the funnel hovering over a community named Sterling City. The policemen immediately determined the cloud's movement—to the southeast, somewhat unusual for such a storm, which usually travels from southwest to northeast. They radioed this information to their headquarters at San Angelo, then began following the funnel: down the valley of the North Concho River (where less than a century earlier had roamed wild buffalo by the thousands but now replaced by cattle, sheep, and goats) and straight toward San Angelo itself. Patrol headquarters alerted several key officials and institutions around the city.

Conveniently for the patrolmen, the funnel seemed to move almost parallel to their highway, at speeds they estimated as being between ten and fifteen miles an hour. Near the city, however, the funnel abruptly changed direction, swooped across the highway less than a block behind the car, and, touching ground, plowed into a northern section called Lake View. For ten minutes that early afternoon of May 11, 1953, from 2:15 to 2:25 P.M., the tornado gouged a path one half mile wide and some three miles long across a residential area, destroying or badly damaging all property it struck: 519 homes, 19 businesses, 150 automobiles. Human casualties included 11 dead, 66 seriously injured, 1,700 homeless.

But the patrolmen's warning had saved lives. Lake View School lay directly in the storm's path, and hundreds of students probably would have become casualties, too (the superintendent said afterward), except for the alert. When that information reached the school, teachers put their pupils through a much-practiced tornado drill. The storm left the building a shambles, but most children were huddled in ground-floor hallways or crouched under desks. Only twelve students were reported injured, none seriously.

Still, drama and terror abounded for them. A seventh grader said later:

> I knew something was going to happen, but I didn't know what. . . . There was a frightening rush of wind. Glass, dust, dirt, sticks—everything seemed to crash into the room and the hall. . . . Then the roof was either sucked off or blew off. . . . The rain came down

on us and we huddled together screaming and crying
. . . but you couldn't hear the crying and screaming for
the wind and the rain.

Elsewhere around the Lake View section, dazed survivors
picked themselves up, surveyed damage, worried about families,
then reacted further in various ways. One woman "cried very
hard . . . [it's] a very desolate feeling to know you don't have
anything left except what you have on your back. We had no insurance on anything we [owned]."

Another woman crept out of an intact closet where she and
her young daughter had sought refuge, stared at the destruction
surrounding her, and, as she recalled later:

> I felt like I was in a different world . . . a strange
> place that I had never been before. . . . When we
> came out there was no sound, there was not a breath of
> air, there was no one in sight, and the whole universe
> had changed.
> . . . I felt like [we were] all alone. I felt like this little
> girl and I were the only people that had survived.
> It's the loneliest feeling in the world—to feel like
> you're the only person left in the place where you've
> lived for several years.

All this was happening that afternoon not even two hundred
miles from us, but we remained in sweet ignorance of it. Further,
and potentially worse for us, San Angelo lay almost directly west
of the ranch, and that would have said something to us about
where the terrible weather might be expected to go, had we
been aware of events. But our thoughts were mostly on suffering
cattle, not people.

Since that Monday, which became more dramatic as the hours
passed, I have read a great deal about tornadoes. Like the
weather proverbs, their history extends back far enough to become lost in the mists of time.

One can only imagine the terror that the violence of a full-
blown tornado would have inspired among primitive, superstitious peoples, with its thunder, lightning, and incredible wind.

The immediate fear could not have been much greater than today's, but an accompanying lack of knowledge about where such a mighty storm had come from and for what purpose, where it was bound, and when the gods or devils would send it back again must have created consternation for a time and remained in memories forever afterward.

One author whose articles on twisters I have read (G. B. Bathurst, writing for *Weather,* 1964) has speculated that the first extant description of a tornado—this one possibly illumined by lightning and colored by whirling sand—might have been recorded about 600 B.C. in Ezekiel 1:4:

> And I looked, and, behold, a whirlwind came out of
> the north, a great cloud, and a fire infolding itself, and a
> brightness was about it, and out of the midst thereof as
> the colour of amber, out of the midst of the fire.

Whatever the truth of the speculation, some early Greek writers did indeed know of and discuss tornadoes—and similar storms at sea, called waterspouts. The latter phenomena actually interested those ancient authors more because of Greece's many maritime ventures.

A Roman author, Lucretius, also wrote on the subject, sometime around 58 B.C., suggesting that lightning might be the energy source for tornadoes. Although Lucretius was said to have been rendered insane by a philter—a potion credited with both magical and sexual powers—he must have formulated his theory during a lucid period. It is one that has also been arrived at, even into the twentieth century, by several observers whose sanity can't be questioned—at least not here and not by name, because some are still living.

Just who penned the first description of a genuine tornado might be debatable, but this is almost certain: those storms have been with mankind since people appeared on earth, and they have returned to plague humanity with a frequency that varies according to location.

An authentic record exists of a tornado that struck London, England, nearly one thousand years ago—on October 17, 1091. It demolished six hundred homes and numerous churches.

Less than fifty years later, in May 1140, a tornado roared into Wellesbourne, Warwickshire, killing a woman and damaging forty houses and a church. "A very violent whirlwind sprang up," wrote a chronicler of the event, "a hideous darkness extended from the earth to the sky. . . ."

In those days of little literacy and poor communication, only a relatively small number of tornadoes were recorded, in England and elsewhere around the world, during the five centuries before a violent storm hit a church at Widecombe-in-the-Moor on October 21, 1638, while the congregation was gathered for worship. High winds and a lightning ball that exploded among worshipers wrecked the building, killed or injured sixty persons, and left survivors feeling sure that the very last day had arrived and that, in fact, they might be in Hell already. Their belief would have been corroborated by a sulfurous smell lingering from lightning bolt and fireball. No doubt it was remindful of brimstone.

One man's death was described by an eyewitness: " . . . his skull [was] rent into three pieces, and his braines throwne upon the ground whole, and the haire of his head, through the violence of the blow first given him, did sticke fast unto the . . . wall of the church; so that hee perished there most lamentably."

Five years after that, in 1643, the first documented tornado struck the American colonies—in Massachusetts—and killed an Indian. Other twisters of early New World record hit New Haven, Connecticut, in 1682, and Charleston, South Carolina, in 1761. The Charleston storm sank five ships in port at the time.

In 1840 a tornado swept across Natchez, Mississippi, and the *Weekly Courier and Journal* carried (in its edition of Friday, May 8, 1840) a story with a tone that would be duplicated in many American newspapers for a long time afterward.

HORRIBLE STORM!!
NATCHEZ IN RUINS!!!

Our devoted city is in ruins, and we have not a heart of stone to detail while the dead remain unburied and the wounded groan for help. Yesterday, at 1 o'clock, while all was peace, and most of our population were at the dining table, a storm burst upon our city and raged for half an hour with most destructive and dreadful power. We look around and see Natchez, yesterday lovely and cheerful Natchez, in ruins and hundreds of our citizens without a shelter or a pillow. Genius cannot imagine, poetry cannot fill up a picture that would match the ruins and distress that every where meets the eye. 'Twas the voice of the Almighty that spoke, and prudence should dictate reverence rather than execration. All have suffered, and all should display the feeling of humanity and the benevolence of religion!

"Under the Hill" presents a scene of desolation and ruin which sickens the heart and beggars description—all, all, is swept away, and beneath the ruins still lay crushed the bodies of many strangers. It would fill volumes to depict the many escapes and heart-rending scenes. . . .

Great numbers of Americans would never become familiar with the most violent of storms, however, until "manifest destiny" had sent them swarming across the Great Plains as travelers or settlers. For reasons that meteorologists could in time explain, conditions on and above those plains are the most favorable of any on earth for the formation of tornadoes, although (as this capsule history of them should have shown) they can appear anywhere, if only rarely in some locations.

Another implication of the universality and age of the tornado lies in a history of that word. The Oxford English Dictionary, the ultimate authority on such a subject, provides these esoterica, in which I have taken the liberty of spelling out words abbreviated in the text.

Tornado . . . In Hakluyt and his contemporaries, *ternado;* from Purchas 1625 onward, *turnado, tournado, tornado.* In none of these forms does the word exist in Spanish or Portuguese. But the early sense makes it probable that *ternado* was a bad adaptation (perhaps originally a blundered spelling) of Spanish *tronada* "thunderstorm" (from *tronar* to thunder), and that *tornado* was an attempt to improve it by treating it as a

derivative of Spanish *tornar* to turn, return. . . . It is notable that this spelling is identified with explanations in
which, not the thunder, but the turning, shifting, or
whirling winds are the main features. . . .

As The Oxford English Dictionary has thus indicated, numerous early writers (and some contemporary ones who live in
relatively calm, quiet parts of the world far removed from
Texas) have used *tornado,* or something similar, when speaking
of thunderstorms. In a 1589 edition of a book compiled by the
Englishman Richard Hakluyt to commemorate and describe notable voyages made by his countrymen, one mariner was quoted
as saying, ". . . we had terrible thunder and lightning, with ex-
ceeding great gusts of raine, called Ternados." In a 1599 edition
another seaman was said to have remarked, "We had nothing
but Ternados, with such thunder, lightning, and raine, that we
could not keep our men drie."

Had those storms been genuine tornadoes, however, the second mariner would have had trouble keeping his men at all, dry
or wet, because when a twister goes to sea and becomes a wa-
terspout it can still blow mightily.

Two other Englishmen, both writers, came closer to describing
a tornado as it would be recognized by most readers today. One
was the poet William Cowper, who was obviously lucid, despite
his occasional bouts with insanity, when he wrote of "Wild tornadoes"—"Wasting towns, plantations, meadows." The other was
Daniel Defoe, an author with a reputation for realism even if he
did make his reputation in pseudohistory, who wrote of "a violent Tournado" that "took us quite out of our Knowledge"—an
emotion that has been shared by many recent victims who have
collected their wits after bombardment by winds that can reputedly reach a velocity as great as five hundred miles an hour.

Against such a storm, man still stands mostly naked, even if he
sometimes won't admit it and even if a few chambers of commerce in tornado-prone areas seek to circumvent the subject.
When a real twister heads his way, even a Finnish wizard must
sprint elsewhere or, if he has tempered his magic with some
practicality, head for the safety of his storm cellar.

But, as might be expected, some people think they can control even the fury of a tornado. Among them are remote descendants of those early (and largely pre-Christian) peoples who shot arrows at oncoming storms with the aim of chasing them off. Some underdeveloped tribes are said to have tried this even into the twentieth century.

With the arrival of gunpowder in the Old World, men who had previously tried and failed with arrows thought they had a better chance to stop threatening clouds. They fired cannon, rifles, and rockets instead. But their lack of success became evident when they resorted to the ringing of church bells, too, as a storm neared. Even this stopped, however, because too many bells were struck by lightning that forked down from a cloud's leading edge. Eventually most weather fighters gave up these tactics, but today in the Po Valley of Italy and in parts of the Soviet Union and Argentina there are said to be contemporary grape growers who have fired skyward many a rocket to protect their vineyards from hail carried by bad storms.

Some South African natives still are tornado fighters. They, too, seem to have enjoyed scant success in past endeavors, even though their "tornadoes" more closely resemble the comparatively mild variety described by those English mariners previously quoted.

When a South African sky becomes ominously darkened by approaching clouds, the tribal magician hurries to a rise nearby and calls for help from his people. After a crowd has assembled, the sorcerer leads his kinsmen in some strange cheers and chants to turn aside the oncoming storm: shouts and wails in imitation of gusting wind, bellows and roars meant to sound like thunder. Thereafter the people fall into a directed silence for a few moments and give their magician the stage for some climactic effort. First comes a piercing, prolonged screech that trails off into a tremulous wail. Then the sorcerer fills his mouth with a magical potion described as foul stuff indeed and spits it contemptuously at the storm.

This routine recommences and continues until the cloud turns aside or roars on into the group, sending everyone fleeing. If it keeps coming despite the sorcery, there *is* an explanation: the magician who sent the storm was more powerful than the one who sought to repulse it.

Another story of mankind's attempt to control storm winds impresses me as being not only more credible but also more tasteful, even considering what happened at the end. Herodotus, a Greek historian of the fifth century B.C., wrote that once upon a time in the land of the Psylli—in northern Africa—a hot, dry, dust-laden wind (called a simoom) blowing from the Sahara dried up the local water supply. Furious inhabitants declared war on the south wind responsible for their plight, formed a mighty army, and marched against it. When they reached the Sahara, that howling red simoom buried in deep sand every last soldier.

3

Still overlooking its propensities, my father and I mentally urged on the great black cloud with that green-tinged base, but now it was obviously veering too far to the north of us. All our entreaties beamed toward that magnificent thunderhead had no more effect than the sorceries of those primitive people.

At this very time, however, some beams of more scientific origin *were* proving effective for their purpose. As I learned later, meteorologists sixty-eight miles southeast of the ranch—at Texas A&M University (then College)—were watching on radar with increasing interest our very thunderstorm. Their transmitter, in operation for less than three months at this time, was sending radio waves flashing far above us, unseen like the winds of lofty elevation that had earlier blown the scurrying cumulus. When those radio waves hit the moisture mass of our cloud, they bounced in all directions, and some of this scattered energy was reflected back to the radar receiver. Thus those distant meteorologists were able to see the same thunderhead we were trying to urge on toward us. They could also ascertain, through intricacies built into their set, the cloud's exact location, distance, and movement. Further than this in regard to radar elucidation I won't go, except to say that I know the word came from a compounding of the phrase *r*adio *d*etecting *a*nd *r*anging, and that I, an ensign newly commissioned from Columbia University Midshipmen's School, dozed off peering into a ship's radarscope one night during World War II while "on watch," as everyone else presumed.

On Texas A&M's radar set the echoes from our cloud were later described by one of the observers as "very intense." Meteorologists began photographing the scope. This was an activity relatively new to them at that time.*

All this occurred more than twenty-three years ago (as I write this), and since then many improvements have been made in electronic weather watching. Still, the old radar set that brought our thundercloud into view that day would have impressed a storm student from an earlier age, Benjamin Franklin, as being something of a miracle.

Until Franklin came along, apparently no one realized the extent of a storm's movement and that the movement did not depend upon surface winds prevailing locally. His discovery of this (a feat less famous than his kite-flying experiment, which proved lightning and electricity to be the same) came accidentally, as has much other knowledge accumulated by the human race. Franklin had intended to observe a lunar eclipse in Philadelphia at 9 P.M., October 21, 1743, but weather prevented. During the day, a storm with whistling northeasterly wind and driving rain struck the city. It continued into evening. No moon became visible, before or after eclipse time.

The disappointed Franklin wrote of this to a brother in Boston, presuming that the same storm had interfered with observations there, too. Considering the northeasterly wind, Franklin,

---

* Air Force meteorologists had preceded them (and other civilian scientists) in wide use of radar for tornado work. By 1953 major air bases in the Midwest were linked by a radar network.

reasoned, the turbulence had blown in from that direction—a common assumption for that day.

When his brother answered, Franklin read the letter with surprise. Residents of Boston, some 250 miles northeast of Philadelphia, had been able to see the eclipse. Weather hadn't closed in, and the storm hadn't struck Boston until much later.

Curiosity about meteorological happenings of that October 21, 1743, superseded Franklin's earlier disappointment. He began reading and collecting weather accounts of that date in newspapers published around the country, and he wrote scientifically minded friends in other localities for supplementary information. As a result, Franklin was able to prove that the storm had struck Philadelphia from the southwest, then had moved on toward the northeast. Later he correctly concluded that storm systems travel a regular course without regard to local breezes and that the northeasterly winds and rains that occasionally buffet Atlantic coastal regions actually come from west and south. All this is commonly known now, thanks largely to a human mind operating entirely without benefit of radar or computers.

In addition to Franklin, many men of remarkable intelligence and curiosity have had roles in the development of meteorology since Aristotle applied Greek philosophy to weather phenomena and produced *Meteorologica*, a work called naïve now, but one recognized as a standard treatise for two thousand years, from about 350 B.C. to A.D. 1650. At least four other individuals are worthy of mention with Franklin and even with Galileo and Torricelli, whose inventions resulted in a great advancement for the science of meteorology beginning in the sixteenth and seventeenth centuries.

One is Henry Piddington, an English mariner who observed in the 1830s that winds of tropical storms in India seemed to revolve, and he called them cyclones, after the Greek *kyklōn*, "whirling." Another is James Pollard Espy, an American scientist who recognized in 1841 the importance of convection (the rising of warm air, its expansion and cooling) in producing storms. A third is Heinrich Wilhelm Dove, a German physicist who observed in the mid-nineteenth century the counterclockwise motion of whirling storms in the Northern Hemisphere (clockwise

in the Southern) and attributed it to the interaction between
tropical and polar air currents. Still another is an American,
Joseph Henry, who collaborated with Espy in setting up the first
telegraphic weather service in the United States, in 1848, four
years after Samuel F. B. Morse sent his famous first telegraph
message, "What hath God wrought!" All this eventually led, in
1870, to the establishment in the United States of a national
weather service. At first it operated under the supervision of the
U. S. Army Signal Corps, because that organization was most intimately involved in telegraphic communication. But in 1880 the
meteorologists were moved to the Department of Agriculture
and given a new name, U. S. Weather Bureau. In 1940 the bureau became part of the Department of Commerce. (Since that
time has come still another change, which will be mentioned
later.)

Those storm-watching meteorologists at Texas A&M possessed
the benefit of all this prior knowledge and work in addition to
their radar set, however antiquated it might seem now, but they
also brought to the job brilliance of their own. Ordinarily I
wouldn't be motivated to remark on their astuteness, having
heard all my life how that college produced only two kinds of
men, fumbling farmers and mostly futile football players, and
having myself graduated from the chief rival academic institution, the University of Texas, which produced not only bright
liberal-arts intellects like myself but also gridiron giants who
could usually crunch A&M skulls one way or another upon the
field of friendly sport. Still, those silent watchers at College Station knew more about that cloud than my father and I, who
stood there with growing disappointment as it moved farther
away to the north.

Those distant meteorologists would have known that this was
only one of 1,800 thunderstorms purportedly growling around
the earth's surface at any given time of day or night. They knew
beyond a doubt that this particular cloud, represented by a mere
blotch on their radarscope, posed a grave threat to areas across
which it swept. They began to suspect the cloud of harboring a
tornado. This guess they based on the appearance of the blotch
on their radarscope, but they also had statistics on their side.

So many twisters have hit Texas, Oklahoma, Kansas, and Missouri that those four states long ago became known as Tornado Alley (a designation since extended all the way to Minnesota). The specific reason for this becomes obvious when one considers in detail something mentioned earlier: the causes of a tornado, as known to contemporary meteorologists.

That type of storm and all other tempests originate within the earth's atmosphere, a gaseous shield protecting life on this planet against deadly radiation, but one that is never as quiet as it appears to an observer on a calm, cloudless day. Heat at the equator and chill at the poles contribute eventually to instability, as do the earth's rotation and still other factors. Differences in temperatures cause differences in atmospheric pressures, and this results in wind: an air flow from areas of high to lower pressure. Direct sunlight warms the air to some extent, but most of the heat comes from the earth's surface, which is heated by the sun. By effecting enormous hot-and-cold exchanges between equator and poles and between lower and upper atmospheric layers, and by a continual release of energy, the storms that develop help to balance the earth's climate while acting also as ecological safety valves.

But if few tornado survivors can see any sort of safety valve in the kind of storm they have lived through, they may be excused. A twister results from air instability that borders on the explosive. Because of the storm's compactness it is more violent than other disturbances. Tornado winds are the strongest known. A hurricane, with its mighty energy extended, will affect a much larger area, one of hundreds of miles, and might blow for a considerable distance with a force of 150 miles an hour or more. On the other hand, the small whirlpool of air called a tornado rarely destroys outside a path extending an eighth of a mile beyond the slim, snakelike, ground-touching funnel that marks its existence. Within the tornado's path, however, ruin is usually complete, for any or all of three reasons. Winds more than twice as violent as the strongest hurricane will batter people and property; or extreme low pressure in the vacuum-like vortex will cause buildings to explode from the normal (but far greater) pressure trapped inside them; or center-of-the-funnel updrafts as great as two hundred miles an hour will carry people and things into the air before lowering the load in various ways.

Scientists still don't know exactly how nature gives birth to such a monster, but they do recognize (as has been indicated) a notable weather condition that greatly favors its generation: a high-moving mass of cold, dry air coming in from west or north-west and overriding warm, moist air blowing up from the south on winds gusting near the surface. Cold air presses down on warm air and prevents its natural inclination to rise, but not for long. Soon, at some spot in the area of cold-hot layers, warm air will force itself upward, and heavier cold air will surge down at that point. Winds blowing horizontally to the surface contribute to tornadic inception by commencing a violent rotary movement around the location of breakthrough, thus forming a vortex, or funnel. Inside the vortex, air pressure drops. If the newly created funnel stays in the sky, it might pass without inflicting damage. In any event it will not be designated a tornado. But if it touches ground, the funnel becomes officially a tornado, in meteorological terms, and it shows its might.

That's one way of describing the origin of a tornado and the capabilities it possesses. Perhaps the description is oversimplified here, but at least parts of it render obvious the reason that certain locations east of the Rocky Mountains have become known as Tornado Alley. Texans, Oklahomans, Kansans, Missourians, and other people nearby happen to have chosen for the enjoyment of life's comforts a region favoring tornado development more than any other part of the world.

Southerly winds blowing near the surface from the tepid Gulf of Mexico carry warm, moist air northward across the central portion of the United States: specifically, across Texas, Oklahoma, Kansas, Missouri, and some bordering states. Meanwhile, another one of those periodic Pacific weather fronts might have begun its invasion of the West Coast, while all that warm, moist air is building up to southeastward. The cold Pacific front characteristically drops most of its moisture on the western slopes of the Rockies before passing on eastward and becoming drier. That's how cold, dry air can seep into skies high above the area to the west of the land called Tornado Alley, which flattens itself out into vast plains over much of its expanse and offers no geographical interference with weather developments overhead.

The cold air pushing in from across Rocky Mountain summits rides over the warm, moist Gulf air, while the entire weather system moves eastward, as usual. Creating still more instability aloft is a giant jet stream flowing in from the Pacific Ocean† and racing eastward across the central plains, stirring the vast weather caldron. From a large weather system, numerous tornadoes may be born about the same time—most of them a hundred miles or more in advance of the line denoting actual location of the cold front.

On the other hand, a tornado might originate from a random thunderhead traipsing through mostly clear skies, if the day is hot and humid and the cloud is significant enough. (A third weather type favoring tornado development is an advancing hurricane, according to Gorden E. Dunn and Banner I. Miller in *Atlantic Hurricanes*.) Tornadoes are about as predictable as lightning, in regard to both exact locations of appearance and results of striking.

One fairly safe prediction can be made, however, on the basis of meteorological history. Certain parts of central Oklahoma probably will have more tornadoes than any other location in the world: more than forty in a ten-year period, as recent statistics have shown. Oklahoma City alone was struck by twenty-six tornadoes during an eighty-year period following 1892.

But all this scarcely approaches an Oklahoma monopoly. Over a span of fifty-two years, from 1916 to 1967, sixteen thousand genuine tornadoes were reported in the New World (as opposed to an earlier total of 150 during a 192-year period from 1682 to 1874, when literate weather observers were few and far between). This total divides into something like 308 twisters a year (virtually all of them in the United States), but the current average for our country is well above that, as will be seen toward the end of Chapter 5. In 1973 alone (said Allen Pearson, meteorologist in charge of the National Severe Storms Forecast Center

† This phenomenon has served at least one other evil purpose. Near the end of World War II, the Japanese used Pacific jet streams to float thousands of bomb-carrying balloons to the United States. Voluntary press censorship prevented panic, although at least 280 bombs hit ground, one as far inland as Iowa. Bomb deaths totaled six—all recorded in Bly, Oregon.

in Kansas City, on NBC's "Today" show, March 8, 1974), observers in forty-six states reported sighting more than 1,100 tornadoes, which would indicate that either those storms have been increasing in number or human eyesight is improving remarkably.

Another recent count, this one covering the thirteen years 1953–65, can give every American who reads this book some idea of his or her chances of being struck by a tornado.

Texas (with the biggest and best of everything, as everyone except out-of-state residents and all honest Texans will agree) naturally leads in tornadoes, too, with an annual average of 109 over that thirteen-year period. Highly buffeted Oklahoma is second, of course, with a 77 average; Kansas third with 72. Only Missouri has proved to be a Tornado Alley disappointment in this particular count, falling to sixth, as this ranking of the other forty-seven states and their yearly tornado averages will show.

4. Nebraska, 39	25. Tennessee, 7
5. Florida, 32	26. Pennsylvania, 6
6. Missouri, 27	Wyoming, 6
7. Illinois, 24	28. Kentucky, 5
Indiana, 24	Massachusetts, 5
9. Iowa, 22	30. Maine, 4
10. South Dakota, 20	Montana, 4
11. Alabama, 18	Virginia, 4
Arkansas, 18	33. Arizona, 3
13. Georgia, 17	California, 3
14. Louisiana, 16	Maryland, 3
15. Colorado, 15	36. Idaho, 2
Michigan, 15	New Hampshire, 2
Minnesota, 15	New York, 2
Wisconsin, 15	39. Connecticut, 1
19. Mississippi, 14	Delaware, 1
North Dakota, 14	New Jersey, 1
21. Ohio, 11	Utah, 1
22. South Carolina, 10	Vermont, 1
23. New Mexico, 9	Washington, 1
24. North Carolina, 8	West Virginia, 1

46. Nevada, less than 1   48. Alaska, 0
       Oregon less than 1   Hawaii, 0
                                                  Rhode Island, 0

Residents of the three states listed at the end aren't guaranteed permanent safety from an occasional tornado by either this author or the National Weather Service—the new name given the U. S. Weather Bureau in 1970, when it became part of the National Oceanic and Atmospheric Administration. The National Weather Service emphasizes that such storms might strike anywhere, but that no tornadoes happen to have been recorded in Alaska, Hawaii, or Rhode Island during the thirteen-year period covered by this particular study.

Why those states should have been exempt from sharing in miseries mutual to many of the rest of us is something I can't explain. Possibly Alaska's earthquakes and winter harshness should excuse it from the additional hazards tornadoes would impose, as might Hawaii's volcanic eruptions and tidal waves. But the only surmise I can make for Rhode Island's good fortune is that the state was too small for tornadoes to find from 1953 to 1965.

Another curiosity (although one not bared in the statistical list just presented) is the absence of tornadoes in the District of Columbia during that period. Maybe nature concluded Washington had been plagued by enough big wind of its own making.

Back on the Texas A&M campus there was an absence of levity. Those observers huddled around their radarscope saw that the thunderstorm had developed an "appendage" (as they called it) sometime around 4:30 P.M. on May 11, 1953. This radarscope phenomenon is more commonly referred to today as a "hook."‡ Whatever it might be called, a trained observer will know its message—a fact acknowledged both now and on that Monday.

The A&M meteorologists were aware that the first tornado actually seen on radar (one observed in Illinois only two months

‡ Its shape on radar is said (by meteorologist Louis J. Battan, in "Killers from the Clouds," *Natural History*, April 1975) to be "apparently caused by raindrops from the parent thunderstorm, which descend in a twisting downdraft and are carried by the winds around the mesocyclone." Battan added that, unfortunately, not all tornadoes show up on radar, and human sighting is still more accurate.

earlier, in March 1953) had exhibited a similar appendage. Although they knew as they watched their own scope "there had been no reports and no evidence of a tornado reaching the ground at this time in this area" (as one man wrote later), they must have suspected they would soon be hearing something. Meanwhile, at that distance and in circumstances then current, they could do little more than look and wait. Today such a radar hook would result in an immediate warning being broadcast on television and radio.

While writing this more than twenty-three years afterward, I am re-examining a photographic print of their radarscope, labeled "1632 CST," or 4:32 P.M. Central Standard Time, May 11, 1953. The appendage is clearly visible protruding from one of several clouds at the upper left of their screen—at a distance eighty miles northwest of them, where it should have been, according to a map I'm also using for reference. If their radar had been able also to show the location of human figures on the ground there would have been, sometime around that moment, two dots visible eighteen miles south of the appendage. Or perhaps my father and I had already left his ranch by that time.

I remember that a rain shower finally fell on us and all that parched earth before we left. After devoting an hour or so to observing clouds moving in from westward, and after watching with dismay while the big one got away to northward, we finally realized with jubilation that other clouds trailing behind the giant thunderhead were traveling on course to reach us. When rain commenced, we took our automobile from the dirt of bare-pasture depths to a firm shoulder of U. S. Highway 81 (now known as I-35), which paralleled the ranch. There we watched happily as the first shower continued to fall on dusty thickets and sunburned vegetation. The cool, damp smell of raindrops carrying moisture to thirsty soil gave off a rich redolence that surpassed any perfume imported from France.

Having looked once more at the "1632 CST" picture of the A&M radarscope, I see the outline of a non-appendaged cloud in the obvious area of our ranch. Maybe that was the one that sent us fleeing from potential pasture mud—or it might have been another shower a short time earlier or later. In any event, we waited alongside U.S. 81 long enough to see that the ranch would indeed get significant relief from the drought that had gripped it for months. Then we drove southward seventeen or eighteen miles to Temple and home.

Ahead of and behind us, as we could clearly see, more scattered showers were closing in. Our windshield wipers threw off the blearing raindrops with regular thumps and scrapes that could be described only as coming with a cheerful rhythm.

4

HAIL AND HIGH WINDS

Less than half an hour later, the menacing sound of hail beating against the roof of my father's house had replaced the happy swish of windshield wipers playing with the first significant rainfall in months.

Upon arrival, during a new downpour, we had left the car near a side entrance and had dashed through the door without any protection against the rain, of course, because we certainly hadn't foreseen such damp developments. After we had toweled dry and had indulged in a few satisfying minutes of rain watching, we noticed the sky blacken again. A late-afternoon spring day that ordinarily would have been aglow with sun full in the west ebbed into seeming nighttide. Soon we heard the hail commence, as suddenly and deliberately as if on signal.

For two or three long minutes we watched ice stones shatter on the concrete driveway, blanket the yellow-green grass of the lawn with what seemed a cover of winter white, rip through west-side awnings erected for protection against that now-vanished setting sun. We could only listen and imagine what the barrage might be doing to the roof.

Then the din lessened, and within seconds a comparative silence returned. Some rain was still falling, we realized, but it came with its usual friendly patter.

Several minutes later, even that stopped. A walk outside to look at the roof proved comforting: no noticeable destruction there (but leaks appeared later, requiring a new layer of composition shingles).

Jangles of the telephone sent us inside again. The call was for me, from the managing editor of the newspaper where I worked. It *was* my day off from work, he acknowledged, but he had heard reports of a tornado striking a community named Hewitt, twenty-six miles north. Would I drive up there and look into it?

The managing editor's request had only one logical answer, especially since I had a wife and a three-month-old son to support. Additionally, my curiosity had been aroused. Hewitt was about twelve miles north of the ranch. The big, black thunderhead we had been summoning silently had moved in that direction. No doubt, it had been the cloud that spawned the tornado, assuming the report was correct. Maybe we had missed something more than rain and hail from that particular storm.

Some hail, we would have accepted gladly, as I've indicated, to get the rain, but I've never had any liking for windstorms. I've always been able to appreciate the purported feelings of early settlers on the Great Plains—that level, treeless surface where wind can still howl as constantly as coyotes once did. This can become grating very quickly, especially when wind blows sand into nostrils and teeth, as it often did during the Dust Bowl era. The historian Walter Prescott Webb surely wrote accurately when he said (in *The Great Plains*), "On the whole, the wind blows harder and more constantly on the Plains than it does in any other portion of the United States, save on the seashore." He and other historians have mentioned the wind's effects on those first settlers. It rubbed men's nerves raw, and it drove some of their women mad.

Any tornado would do even worse, of course, but its coming isn't usually heralded by wind, but by a period of oppressive calm: several hours or days of uncomfortably warm, humid weather, when a wind (if there is one) might seem to blow from a heated furnace. Under those conditions, dark clouds of odd colors moving in from the west become truly ominous. The day can assume a look almost of night, and the sky might seem to boil with clouds black, purple, green, gray, and white. Usually this awesome display is accompanied by flashes of lightning and crashes of thunder: by those livid streaks that represent electrical discharges from one cloud to another or from a cloud to earth, and by the ensuing roar resulting from an explosive expansion of air heated by the stroke. Occasionally two cloud masses will collide and create a tumult in the heavens: lightning followed by a thunderclap, then a wild display of atmospheric confusion as clouds swoop earthward or shoot skyward.

The result of all this might be only rain, hail, and a windstorm. It might also be a tornado, if the clouds commence showing a rotation. Out of that, a funnel can develop. Usually it will first look steamy white or gray because of condensation of water vapor. Additional moisture might darken it and make the usual display of interlaced lightning more spectacular. After touching ground, the funnel virtually always takes on a terrifyingly black appearance from the loose earth and debris drawn up into it.

Observers have described some funnels as having the appearance of an elephant's trunk swaying back and forth. This is an appropriate description, because a tornado can suck up water (and almost anything else in its path) the same as can an elephant. Other reported funnels have resembled ropes, snakes, hourglasses, wedges, vertical columns, balloons, and kite tails—all extending from clouds. Often they make their approach accompanied by rain and hail, and always with a fearful roar that can make it impossible to hear a brick building collapse. Little else can be said, however, that would characterize tornadoes generally.

Wondering what I would find from the one that had struck Hewitt, I grabbed notebook, pencil, and camera (because our newspaper staff size frequently demanded combined duties), squeezed behind the steering wheel of my car, and drove back up U.S. 81 toward the ranch. Rain had stopped and clouds had broken, allowing much more late-afternoon daylight to permeate the countryside. But water still stood in puddles on highway shoulders and in plowed fields that had until recently sent dust billowing skyward on windy days.

A tornado. Although I was a resident of Tornado Alley, those storms really inspired no great fear in me then, because I had escaped close association with them. One reason was that I hadn't always been a Texas resident. True, I had lived my first twelve years in wind-blown Abilene, where my father taught English and started the intercollegiate track-and-field program at Abilene Christian College (now University). But in 1937 we moved to Los Angeles, California, and I grew up there (although some of my classmates at Horace Mann Junior High and George Washington High School might still dispute that word choice). After World War II, I attached myself to Southern California institutions of higher learning ranging in size from Pepperdine College (now also University) to U.C.L.A. before returning more or less permanently to Texas.

Since that May 11 nearly a quarter of a century ago, however, Texas weather has generously afforded me closer looks at those storms often referred to as "twisters." Consequently, after viewing one extraordinary example of tornado devastation and after living through three near misses (a matter of ten blocks or so) that were foretold by broadcasts and by wails of civil defense sirens, my respect for their destructive capability has zoomed.

Further, since that day, I have read about and talked with tornado survivors who have told some stories that are vivid enough for me as secondhand narratives. (May they always remain in that category.) These narratives I have collected, and I have chosen at random seven accounts to use here, as eyewitness descriptions of how a tornado looks and sounds, and what it does.

One is an account of a tornado that struck Spruce Creek Valley, in the central Pennsylvania Alleghenies, in the early 1870s, as seen and described for posterity in an old journal article by a clergyman named J. B. Meek. The account was so detailed that contemporary meteorologists gave it particular attention then as a good discourse on the birth and life of a tornado.

Meek's residence was situated on the south side of the valley, which ran in a southwesterly direction between two mountains— one named Tussey's, to the northwest, and another named Bald Eagle, to the southeast. On the day of the storm, the Meeks had as guest in their home a male friend. About noon the man prepared to return, horseback, to his own residence, in Stone Valley, southward beyond Bald Eagle Mountain, which he would have to cross. Meek decided to go with him.

The morning had been "close," with uncomfortable humidity. Mrs. Meek, a woman of obvious intuition, suggested that her husband and his friend carry umbrellas and overcoats: ". . . she was sure, from the feeling of the atmosphere, that a storm was impending." The two men agreed, mounted horses, and departed —about twelve-thirty. Hard climbing combined with oppressiveness of the air made the ascent of Bald Eagle extremely slow and arduous.

When they had completed two thirds of their climb to the crest, they heard thunder rumbling off to the northwest and saw there the flickers of distant lightning, but their sight of the storm itself was cut off by Tussey's Mountain, which loomed in between. Unable to hurry, they continued their climb while thunder boomed uncomfortably louder.

At the summit, Meek and his friend saw the storm: " . . . a dark . . . cloud at a distance of about eight or nine miles" spread out over "15 or 20 degrees of the horizon." Ensuing description, as Meek left it, was detailed; it has been compressed here:

> [The cloud] exhibited such . . . [a] threatening appearance that we almost involuntarily remained stationary, as if spell-bound by the phenomenon. It was very dense, and strangely agitated by a rapid vertical commotion near the middle of the mass, while it was . . . traversed with discharges of electricity in different directions, mostly vertically, accompanied [by] heavy peals of thunder. Its direction . . . was diagonally across the valley from . . . northwest to . . . southeast.

As it came over the crest of the opposite mountain it
. . . seemed to precipitate itself suddenly down the
slope . . . and almost instantly to hide from our view
all objects on that side of the valley; as it came near
. . . we perceived that . . . the cloud . . . consisted of a
violent and very rapid shooting upward in the middle,
turning outward and downward on the exterior columns
of mist. . . . The whole presented the appearance of a
boiling caldron violently agitated. . . .

Meek also described the movement of the tornado: "exceedingly rapid." He estimated the storm traveled fifteen miles in less
than thirty minutes, leaving a clean path through heavily
wooded land. All the while, as he and his friend stood watching,
there came a sound "like that of the Falls of the Niagara," punctuated by continuous thunderclaps. The spectacle reminded
Meek of "an immense locomotive-engine passing rapidly over the
valley, belching forth smoke and steam." At one site, the tornado
struck a mill pond and sucked it dry, "even throwing up from the
bottom sticks and stones which had long been sunk in the mud."
Then the storm roared out of Spruce Valley: across a ridge and
into another depression on the other side. There it plowed another path twenty miles long, Meek learned later.

Seventeen years later, a U. S. Weather Bureau meteorologist
witnessed a tornado, in April 1888, near Abilene, Texas, where
he was stationed. The weatherman was Isaac Cline, who would
later be serving as local forecast official at Galveston when, in
1900, a hurricane struck that coastal city and claimed some six
thousand lives. Cline wrote of his experience with the tornado:

. . . While driving along a roadway formed by wire
fencing, about three miles from Abilene, I heard a
terrific roaring noise behind me. Looking around I saw
a tornado with its funnel-shaped cloud swirling in the
air and traveling parallel to the road and only about
two hundred yards away from the road. The tornado
was traveling at a speed of about ten miles per hour
while the wind velocity in the swirling storm was so
great that it could not be measured. I stopped and

watched the tornado so that if it should take up a course towards me I could turn and go in an opposite direction and escape.* As it crossed Lytle Creek it carried the water up in a solid stream. It tore mesquite trees up by the roots and whirled them about in the air like feathers. The column connecting the funnel cloud with the earth became overextended and parted about one-fourth of a mile above the ground. [When that happened,] the water which was carried up out of Lytle Creek poured down on the earth and washed out a large hole in the ground. The funnel cloud continued to swirl in the clouds . . . and again reached down to the ground about two miles farther to the east.

Twenty-eight years before Cline's experience, a Kansas man by the name of Weisbard also had witnessed a tornado and had written a description of it. His report, too, received the careful attention of meteorologists of that day.

Weisbard owned a store in Marysville, Kansas, in 1860. On Tuesday, July 31, of that year, with the thermometer riding at 102 degrees and a brisk breeze blowing from the south, a dark cloud appeared in the northwest, up the valley of the Big Blue River. Weisbard watched it change "into a dark gray cylindrical mass of vapor." The storm swept down the valley in the direction of Marysville, unroofing houses, uprooting trees, carrying away fences and even vegetables growing in gardens and fields. The time was 3:30 P.M.

When [the tornado] struck . . . Marysville it filled the air with dust and a dark mass of clouds, until it seemed like midnight. The first crash burst in the front door of my store, and then carried the roof off. I went out the back door to save my trunk, when the wind hurled me S[outh], towards my stable, where I grasped an elm post, around which I was several times whipped, but managed to hold on until the storm was over. A [man] . . . was [blown] from my side and carried several hun-

---

* These days a motorist would be well advised to speed off at a right angle to the storm, if roads allow it.

dred feet over the ruins of a house and deposited in
Spring Creek Valley. On the prairies in the center of the
storm track, the grass was completely stripped, as in
winter after the prairie fires. . . .

Weisbard's companion who had been "carried several hundred
feet . . . and deposited in Spring Creek Valley" would have had
a story to tell, too, assuming he had lived, but apparently he
didn't leave it for posterity. I have, however, read an account
that would have been similar to, and no doubt as incredible as,
that man's experience. The story, distributed by the Associated
Press, was datelined Wichita Falls, Texas; the clipping I have is
from the Houston *Post* of April 3, 1966, two years after the event
described.

Roy Bennett, a master sergeant at Sheppard Air Force Base,
near Wichita Falls, was at home on the afternoon of April 3,
1964, watching through a living-room window the development
of ominous weather to westward. Nearby, his wife, Dorothy,
looked on, too. Their two children were still in school.

About 2:50 P.M. Bennett saw a black funnel come into view,
headed their way. He told his wife to get his parents, who lived
next door, and flee the area. Then he and his sister and brother-
in-law (identified as Mr. and Mrs. E. Caswell, visitors from San
Antonio) walked into the front yard for a better view. A sudden
hailstorm drove them back inside, and they sought the best refuge possible from a tornado that now seemed certain to strike.
Bennett leaped behind a heavy piece of furniture, a combination
television-high-fidelity set, and the Caswells crouched under a
kitchen table.

Bennett heard what seemed to be many bricks hitting his
house and a roar like "a hundred freight trains," which soon became even louder. He grasped the combination set and watched
as a garbage can crashed through his picture window; then he
saw, beyond the shattered opening, house trailers flying through
the air. From a window of one trailer an elderly woman and a
dog stared out in terror. Moments later their vehicle slammed
into Bennett's residence, cutting through two bedrooms.

A blowing door gave Bennett a bloody gash across the top of

his head, but he remained conscious. Just as a deathly stillness settled upon the house, he saw a pane of glass disintegrate in midair near him.

The sudden silence led him to speculate that the small eye of the storm had arrived. He must have been right: the calm was only momentary. When the roaring recommenced, he saw his sister hurled against kitchen cabinets only seconds before a wall collapsed on her. She and her husband died. Bennett felt his own grip around the heavy piece of furniture loosening, realized the tornado was about to pull him from the house, and grasped some exposed bathroom pipes with such force that (as he learned later) he broke several bones in his left hand.

Hurtling debris again filled the air. Something apparently struck him and caused him to loosen his hold, because, as he said, "The next thing I knew, I was circling upward, inside the funnel."

With remarkable clarity Bennett remembered later many details of his incredible flight. The funnel, about three feet in diameter, carried him steadily upward, along with a tractor, some automobile tires and fenders, and a bed with mattress and covers intact—all circling in orbits near him. "If I could just get close enough to that bed," he later recalled thinking, "I'd lie down and sleep." At a height he estimated as 250 feet he looked down at the ground—down through the narrow, all-dominating funnel—and he saw the tornado sweeping more destruction far below.

Circling winds began to lower him, but they were only teasing. After a time, he found that he had been carried even higher. Then his consciousness waned. He next recalled lying entangled in a roll of barbed wire 150 feet from his home.

He was an unrecognizable, swollen mass of torn flesh and broken bones. When searchers finally realized his identity, he was taken to Sheppard Air Force Base Hospital and given last rites there by a priest. But he lived instead, and twenty months later he walked out of the place with a discharge, a 90 per cent disability pension, and, no doubt, a silent entreaty that his close association with tornadoes might be forever ended.

A similar plea would have been expressed by a Kansas farmer who once looked up into a funnel rather than down through it.

Will Keller, who lived near Greensburg, described his experience
for Dodge City weatherman A. A. Justice, who prepared the account for publication in the *Monthly Weather Review* of May
1930.

> On the afternoon of June 22, 1928, between three and
> four o'clock, I noticed an umbrella-shaped cloud in the
> west and southwest and from its appearance suspected
> there was a tornado in it. The air had that peculiar op-
> pressiveness which nearly always precedes . . . a tor-
> nado.

Keller continued to examine the cloud and quickly realized he
was right. He saw three funnels dropping earthward from a
green-tinged black base. One of them seemed to be headed in
the direction of his farmhouse. He hurried home, alerted his family, and took them to a storm cellar nearby. No rain was falling,
so Keller tarried at the doorway to take a last look before following the others inside the shelter.

> . . . The great shaggy end of the funnel hung directly
> overhead. Everything was still as death. There was a
> strong, gassy odor, and it seemed as though I could not
> breathe. There was a screaming, hissing sound coming
> directly from the end of the funnel. I looked up, and to
> my astonishment I saw right into the heart of the tor-
> nado. There was a circular opening in the center of the
> funnel, about fifty to one hundred feet in diameter and
> extending straight upward for a distance of at least half
> a mile, as best I could judge. . . . The walls of this
> opening were [composed of] rotating clouds and the
> whole was brilliantly lighted with constant flashes of
> lightning, which zigzagged from side to side. Had it not
> been for the lightning, I could not have seen the open-
> ing, or any distance into it.
> Around the rim of the great vortex small tornadoes
> were constantly forming and breaking away. These
> looked like tails as they writhed their way around the
> funnel. It was these that made the hissing sound. I no-

ticed the rotation of the great whirl was [counterclock-
wise], but some of the small twisters rotated clockwise. The opening was entirely hollow, except for
something I could not exactly make out but suppose it
was a detached wind cloud. This thing kept moving up
and down. . . .

Keller's and Bennett's stories, as incredible as they are, are not
much more astounding than any of a number of other accounts I
have collected. They differ only in details, almost all of them
amazing. Each tornado seems to have the uniqueness of an individual fingerprint.

Some stories are amusing—a credit in this respect to the
human courage and resilience as well as to the sense of humor of
survivors who told them. For instance, there's the story of 84-
year-old L. W. Box of Drumright, Oklahoma, as clipped from the
Drumright *Journal* of July 25, 1974, and sent to me by one of
Box's friends.

Box, who traces his ancestry back to Basques inhabiting the
northern provinces of Spain, was living alone in Drumright on
the afternoon of June 8, 1974. (His wife died in 1967; their only
child, Paul, was killed in Burma during the Second World War.)
Since Box preferred an early evening meal, he had cooked a light
supper and brewed coffee by 5 P.M. that day.

A tornado alert interrupted him. Box told the rest of the story.

I went out to the front porch . . . but I couldn't see
anything so I went back to the kitchen to eat. I had just
sat down when I heard [a] noise and decided it was
time to get to the basement. . . . I [had just] got inside
when "Whish!" the basement [door] lifted off and blew
away. I stepped back in[to] the corner of the basement
in case of things blowing in.

From my window in the basement I could see . . .
three houses . . . lift off and blow away. . . .

After things quieted down, I came back up and as I
passed through the kitchen, I picked up my cup of
coffee and went out front to see what happened. . . .
As I got out there one of my neighbors came running

up to see if I was all right and saw me standing there
with a cup of coffee in my hand. He told me if he
hadn't . . . been so glad to see me, he would have
poured that . . . coffee down my neck.

One of the calmest and most amusing tornado accounts I
know of, however, is a personal-experience story told on tape for
me by Box's friend who sent that clipping. She is Mrs. Pearl
Pruitt, a widow now living in Ponca City, Oklahoma, but in 1956
a resident of the southwestern section of Box's town, Drumright.

On the evening of April 2 of that year Mrs. Pruitt, who had
become a schoolteacher after the death of her husband, was enjoying the last day of Easter vacation, although the day was
cloudy, sultry, and a bit "depressing." It was a Monday.

After returning home from a dinner party, she pinned her hair,
cleaned her dentures and left them in the bathroom, then decided to read for a while before going to bed. Local forecasts
had mentioned the possibility of tornadoes in the area, but no
effective warning system had been developed then.

Her light flickered and went out. "How unusual!" she thought.
It was the first time in the thirty years she had lived in
Drumright that "OG&E" electricity had failed.

But Oklahoma Gas and Electric was reliable, she reflected.
The light would be back on soon. She put her book on a marble-
topped table nearby and sat in gloominess awaiting the moment.

When the light came back on, she picked up her book, but almost immediately another flicker forewarned of returning darkness. She stared at the bulb as its brightness waned: "It faded
down to a little dot like the TV screen does when you turn off a
program."

Still, she awaited the return of OG&E power. This time,
hower, there was no resurgence. Resigning herself to continued
darkness, she felt for the light switch and turned it to the "off"
position, found her way into the adjoining bedroom, and pulled
up the covers around her.

The roar of "a huge airplane" coming continually closer dis-
turbed her. It seemed even to be pulling bobby pins from her
hair. She realized then that so large a plane probably wouldn't

be flying low over her house, especially at that hour. "This is a storm," she concluded. "I'd better pray."

Her house began disintegrating: like crackers being crushed in human hands, she thought. "I could only think of to pray, 'God's will be done,'" she remembered later. She repeated this entreaty two or three times, then had a feeling of whirling through the air. She thought for a moment her head would be twisted from her body.

Following this came a sensation of dropping, then of lying on something solid. Her first thought was that the tornado had pushed her off the far side of her bed, into a space of eighteen inches or so that she always left between mattress and bedroom wall.

"Well, the storm didn't kill me," Mrs. Pruitt mused as she lay caught and cramped within the folds of her bed covers and her mattress. "I'll run across the street to my neighbor's." Reflection later evoked wonder as to why she thought the other residence would have been intact, but at the moment of the storm's departure her first impulse was "to get out of here."

A second impulse replaced the first. Mrs. Pruitt could still hear a distant roar, and she recalled listening to stories of Tornado Alley residents who emerged too soon from cellars and other shelters and were struck by flying debris. "I must stay here," she concluded, but her wait was long and impatient.

Finally silence returned. She tried to get out, only to discover that she couldn't move or breathe easily. "Isn't this a sight!" she thought. "The storm didn't kill me, but I'll smother to death."

> About then I heard my young neighbor second door north of me calling to his wife. I knew I must let him know where I was, so I could get out of there. My voice never was very strong, and it took me [several] attempts for him to hear me.
>
> He answered, "Pearl, where are you?" I said I was in my bedroom—where I thought I was. But I guess he could tell by my voice I wasn't where my bedroom was. I was across the street [as I discovered later].
>
> He got me on my feet. He kept saying, over and over, "Pearl, I don't see how you're alive."

By then Mrs. Pruitt had realized the extent of her fortune. Apparently during that whirling period the wind had wrapped her mattress—"a large, heavy Beautyrest"—around her body and had covered her face with blankets, giving her that fear of smothering, but at the same time providing protection.

She answered her distraught neighbor, seeking to console him, "Well, you can see I'm alive. . . . I'm not hurt. You see, God just wrapped that mattress around me and made a protective shelter for me." Later, however, she became aware of a few injuries: painful bruises and bloody knees.

Mrs. Pruitt saw well enough in the gloom to know that her home, across the street, had been demolished: "not a board left standing." She wondered what had happened to all the bricks in it. Some certainly should have hit her, she reasoned, during her airborne period; yet the only ones she ever became aware of (and identified as being from her residence) were two or three bricks deeply embedded in the earth on which her home had stood. "What [part of my house] wasn't just swept with the wind for miles . . . was left in the middle of the street, and cars couldn't get through there."

She was still in a condition of shock, whether or not anyone else realized it, when another neighbor appeared and offered to drive her out of the wrecked area—anywhere she wanted to go.

Reflecting on that choice, she silently decided that her first preference would be to replace her lost dentures. She had a woman friend in Drumright, a fellow teacher, who had recently acquired a third set of false teeth, and she hoped that with luck they might prove wearable in her own mouth. She asked her neighbor to take her to the friend's house. Before leaving her neighborhood, she saw a few looters already at work, along with many rescuers.

At the schoolteacher's residence, in an undamaged part of town, she quickly discovered the impossibility of using the other dentures. When her school principal happened along, checking on the well-being of his teachers, she prevailed on him to drive her back to the site of her demolished home.

"Why do you want to go back there?" the principal asked, obviously reluctant to take his car and perhaps the immaculate suit he was wearing into that part of town.

"Because I want my little strongbox," Mrs. Pruitt answered. Dentures first, but other valuables a quick second.

"Why, Mrs. Pruitt, you'll never find it. Where did you have it?"

"In my refrigerator."

"In your refrigerator? Why did you put it there?"

"Because I was afraid of fire, and I knew that would never burn."

After stalling for a few more minutes, the principal finally helped her into his car and took her home. Near the devastated area he parked, then walked with her to the site of her residence.

"Where do you want me to start looking?" he asked, possibly stifling some feeling of exasperation.

"See if you can find the refrigerator," Mrs. Pruitt said.

Years afterward, she reflected with wonder at her demands, which, she felt, were not typical of her. "It didn't occur to me that I could look for anything. I just stood there telling others what to do."

The principal, attired in a "spick and span" suit, began combing debris. He uncovered an old electric refrigerator with a spiral motor on top, retrieved an object from it, and walked over to Mrs. Pruitt. She noticed milk running down his otherwise spotless coat and shirt, but with great satisfaction heard him proclaim, "Here it is."

He drove her back to the home of her schoolteacher hostess. Soon friends who had heard of the disaster began dropping in, bringing necessities like clothes to replace her losses, which (even if insured) included everything. But still she had no teeth, and she expressed a desire to look for them, too, in the aftermath of the strongbox success.

That night, from her friend's house, she called relatives in Ponca City to report herself alive. She added that her home was gone, and so were her dentures. A plea to a nephew that he bring a new set as soon as he could evoked a promise from him to oblige.

Mrs. Pruitt went to bed then, but not to sleep. When, about 2 or 3 A.M., her friend's son arrived from Norman, where he attended the University of Oklahoma and had learned of the tornado, Mrs. Pruitt heard her hostess say that she had a guest, Pearl Pruitt, who wanted someone to help look for her dentures in the morning.

"She'll never find them," the young man answered.

"I know, but she thinks she will. Try, anyway."

At daylight the three of them drove over to the site of Mrs. Pruitt's shattered house.

"Where shall I start looking?"

"Don't step on a board!" Mrs. Pruitt answered, again in her unusual, imperious manner. "They might be under it. You lift every board until you find my teeth."

Another lengthy search ensued. After a time Mrs. Pruitt heard her helper exclaim, "Here are your uppers!"

Wonderful, she thought. "They are the most important!" She saw that they were intact, although covered with dirt.

A neighbor appeared about that time and asked if she needed any help. "I thought it a foolish question," Mrs. Pruitt reflected later, "but I finally said, 'Here, you can clean my teeth.'"

Within moments the searcher called out from amid the debris, "Well, here are the lowers!"

"Fine! I knew you'd find them."

Mrs. Pruitt turned to her helpful neighbor and added, "Take these, too." A short time later she had her dentures back, cleaned and carefully transported on a pink Kleenex. She put them in her mouth immediately and "hardly took them out for ever so long." When telling the story, eighteen years later (in July 1974), she was wearing the same dentures and wouldn't have traded them for a newer set.

But her story continued after the discovery of those lost teeth. If she seemed imperious during the search for her strongbox and dentures, it was a momentary change of personality. Her calm in the wake of personal disaster, her rejection of self-pity, and her gratitude for help given became recognized around Drumright.

People were wonderful to me—both those in Drumright and [elsewhere]. Someone from far away sent our church $100. They gave it to me. I got so many clothes the teachers would greet me every morning with: "Here comes our best-dressed teacher. I wonder whose clothes she's wearing today?"

That tornado helped me to see the kindness of people. They gave not only clothes, but also jewelry, towels, sheets, pillow cases, and money.

I just can't describe the kindness of people.

On the other hand, many individuals who knew Mrs. Pruitt were unable to account for her serenity in days and weeks immediately following the disaster. After school recommenced, she would take the first graders to her home site for "show and tell" and describe for them what happened to her when the tornado hit. Later, when visiting the homes of a few acquaintances and noticing articles that once belonged to her—items obviously retrieved from debris by the new owners after some deliberate sifting—she masked her disappointment and anger with silence, and she continued to commend the helpfulness of all those around her.

"People couldn't understand how I took it so calmly," she said eighteen years later, "but my faith meant everything to me."

She never questioned the answer given her storm-motivated prayer. As she would emphasize afterward to any cynic who doubted the rationality of her continued faith, she hadn't prayed that her personal safety be assured or that her property be spared—simply that "God's will be done." For anyone (atheists excepted) in the direct path of a tornado like the one whose devastation I was soon to become aware of, on May 11, 1953, four words of greater logic would be hard to compose.

5

SCATTERED WRECKAGE

At Hewitt, the community reportedly struck by a tornado, I found much mud, a water-soaked dog lying dead near a large tree against which it had been blown, downed utility poles, a few wrecked automobiles, some damaged buildings, and a number of extremely talkative residents. But if the storm had left them terrified, they didn't show it as they spoke in that lazy-sounding drawl then common among rural folk in our part of the country.

In those days Hewitt was an undeveloped country village of perhaps two hundred inhabitants, situated just west of U.S. 81 and seven or eight miles south of the downtown section of the largest city in our vicinity, Waco. Not much stood in Hewitt for a tornado to shatter, but such a statement as that, publicly declared, would only have alienated residents with whom I talked that day.

One man told me that a Mr. and Mrs. O. D. Evans had been taken to a Waco hospital suffering from injuries. They had been sitting in their living room as the storm neared. When the roar became intense, they clung together until the house blew away. They were carried with it.

Other stories unfolded. One man, Floyd Denard, saved himself by diving into a ditch just as wind picked up the truck he was driving, carried it a hundred yards, and left it wrecked. A ten-year-old boy, Ronald McLemore, told a tale of similar terror. He and his father had been driving west from their residence to the family farm when the tornado roared in. Wind gusts became terrifying, and the darkness seemed like night, but they hadn't heard of any storm warnings and presumed this would be just heavy rain. Three quarters of a mile from home, the weather became so bad Ronald's father tried to pull into a residence driveway. Poor visibility caused him to miss the entrance. The automobile rolled into a ditch, and mud held it there. From inside the car they watched as large pieces of metal blew past "like cardboard."

After the tornado had whirled on elsewhere, young McLemore and his father surveyed the damage. The first thing Ronald noticed was the absence of any roofing over the small depot of the Missouri, Kansas, and Texas Railroad—the "Katy" stop at Hewitt. Not far away, a 35-foot semaphore stood "twisted like a pretzel." Then Ronald heard someone shout, "The Evans house is gone!" In time it became clear that Mr. and Mrs. Evans were the only persons injured and their home the only one demolished.

I looked over the scattered wreckage, glanced again at the dead dog, and prepared to return. A funnel had indeed touched ground there, but there wasn't much of a story to write—even though the residents of 1953 Hewitt would likely remember this day for the rest of their lives.

Just then, a man volunteered information that I should go on to Waco. He said the tornado had struck that city, too. How he acquired this information that day is something that has puzzled me ever since. Communications in the vicinity were notably poor, I discovered as the evening progressed, and many persons who resided almost next door to disaster remained unaware of events until the following morning. Possibly the man had just driven in from the city, but I don't recall his saying that.

I don't remember calling the newspaper at that time, either, but I must have. Then I drove back to U.S. 81—the best route then—and on toward Waco. New clouds hovering over a gloomy western horizon darkened the early evening.

A course toward Waco would have been normal indeed for any tornado that hit Hewitt, which lay south of and slightly west of the city. As mentioned, tornadoes commonly come from a southwesterly direction—a fact I knew even then, before I had begun collecting information on those monsters. As is true of almost everything about tornadoes, however, no one can be certain of this. Most of the storms usually strike in midafternoon, too, but they have been known to sneak up on sleeping people in the earliest hours of morning and leave them wondering what happened.

Providing descriptions of various twisters is a *Report on the Character of Six Hundred Tornadoes* that occurred from 1794 through 1881, published by the United States Government in 1884. "Direction of storm's course" is given for 384 of those tornadoes. According to my examination of the records, a total of 325, or nearly 85 per cent, came from the southwest. Of the rest, 44 came from northwest, 15 from due west. Possibly some of the latter observations were faulty. The direction might have been from slightly south (or north) as well as west.

The earliest recorded tornado on that list, one that struck Northford, Connecticut (eight or nine miles northeast of present downtown New Haven) at 4 P.M. on June 19, 1794, came from the usual direction, southwest. The funnel looked more like an hourglass, observers said, but its effect on touching ground was the same as more conventional funnels. Traveling through the village, it swept clean a path from one hundred to three hundred feet wide. Extremely sultry weather preceded the cloud. The storm itself hit immediately after the populace had been awed by lightning described as "illuminated and glowing" and frightened by heavy rain and hail.

Another notation provided additional description of this tornado: "Progress rapid; on each side of path almost a dead calm;

cloud alternately contracted and expanded" as it prowled northeastward.

To re-emphasize, not every tornado moves in from the southwest, or even from northwest or west. An Oklahoma storm that plowed through Caddo County, southwest of Oklahoma City, on June 2, 1949, left a path of destruction that from the air appeared to describe a perfect circle, with a diameter of about two miles. Five years before that, a similarly erratic June tornado struck the northwestern Iowa county of Sioux—on the sixteenth of the month. For as long as twenty minutes, the tornado remained stationary. Then it began moving: to the southeast, south, east, and north before finally disappearing in an easterly direction, having completed what could be called a U turn.

The occurrence of a tornado remaining in one place for so long was as unusual as the odd turns it made. The storms virtually always move across the countryside with considerable haste, although they don't commonly stretch their destruction over a great distance. Most tornadoes advance at speeds of from twenty to thirty miles an hour, although some have been recorded as slow as five and some as fast as sixty-five miles an hour.

The *Report on the Character of Six Hundred Tornadoes* included a column entitled "Shortest time in passing a point." Although such information was rarely available, scattered entries afford some idea of the suddenness with which a tornado can strike and pass on—even though a survivor might think time went into limbo during the storm's peak. Two 1878 tornadoes—at Richmond, Missouri, June 1, and near Albany, New York, July 21—hit and left in ten seconds. An August 22, 1851, storm at West Cambridge, Massachusetts, required sixteen seconds for passage. A May 23, 1878, tornado at Mineral Point, Wisconsin, took eighteen seconds. Usually, however, the ordeal for persons caught lasts longer, as this list of a dozen random tornadoes (excerpted from the same report) will show:

PLACE AND DATE	MINUTES (′) OR SECONDS (″)
Collinsville, Illinois, April 14, 1879	2′
Erie County, Ohio, July 11, 1879	5′

Irving, Kansas, May 30, 1879	40″
Laconia, Indiana, February 21, 1878	1–2′
Las Cruces, New Mexico, September 10, 1875	10′
Macon, Mississippi, April 25, 1880	3′
Memphis, Tennessee, June 17, 1877	3½′
Monroe County, Georgia, March 20, 1875	50″
Rushford, New York, July 25, 1838	40″
Savoy, Texas, May 28, 1880	2′
Suffield, Connecticut, May 29, 1880	8′
Walterboro, South Carolina, April 16, 1879	40″

Some other tornadoes were so slow in passing that survivors must have thought their ordeal covered hours, not mere minutes. A tornado that struck Milford, Pennsylvania, October 30, 1875, hung on for half an hour. Two other storms, both in New York State, whirled and roared for at least twenty minutes in one place: at Vernon Center July 10, 1878, and in Onondaga County July 30, 1879. Another 1879 tornado struck Winnemucca, Nevada, nine days before Christmas and lasted fifteen minutes before giving victims any respite—not a great length of time, maybe, except for persons caught in such violence in a region that ordinarily suffers little from tornadoes and at a time of year when comparatively few of them develop anywhere.

The short, narrow paths they usually sweep out can also fluctuate. A funnel might dip from the sky, destroy a single object, and lift without doing further damage. On the other hand, it might plow a furrow 293 miles long, as one tornado did, on May 26, 1917. The funnel touched down at the town of Louisiana, on the Mississippi River in northeastern Missouri, roared through central Illinois and crashed into the town of Mattoon, then entered Indiana and almost traversed that state before lifting at the eastern edge of Jennings County, some forty miles west of Cincinnati. That was the longest continuous tornado ever recorded at that time.

Paths of vicious ones today may usually be measured in a matter of a score of miles, at most. But tornadoes that cut swaths many miles long are not, and never were, remarkable, as shown by this random list of twelve tornadoes again taken from that

Report on the Character of Six Hundred Tornadoes. (Many, but not all, towns mentioned were at or near the point of origin. In every case, however, the locality lay in the tornado's path.)

PLACE AND DATE	LENGTH OF PATH, IN MILES
Harrison, Ohio, February 14, 1854	50
Lee's Summit, Missouri, May 30, 1879	86
Marshfield, Missouri, April 18, 1880	120
Mineral Point, Wisconsin, May 23, 1878	150
New Brunswick, New Jersey, June 19, 1835	17½
New Harmony, Indiana, April 30, 1852	250
North Platte, Nebraska, vicinity, June 25, 1881	140
Nottoway, Virginia, July 13, 1876	35
Pike County, Alabama, March 18, 1880	20
Richmond County, Georgia, March 20, 1875	185
Saline County, Kansas, June 6, 1876	40
Sunapee, New Hampshire, September 9, 1821	20

Paths usually aren't wide, although they may range up to two miles, from a minimum width of one hundred feet or less. Another random sampling from that *Report* will give an idea of the width range.

PLACE AND DATE	MAXIMUM WIDTH OF PATH, IN FEET
Andrew County, Missouri, June 12, 1881	1,200
Biloxi, Mississippi, August 22, 1879	100
De Soto Parish, Louisiana, November 9, 1880	800
Fargo, [North] Dakota, August 26, 1878	5,000
Florence, Arizona, July 31, 1878	8,000
Galesburg, Illinois, vicinity, August 5, 1875	1,200
Harrison, Ohio, February 14, 1854	600
Indianola, Texas, July 11, 1877	200
Mineral Point, Wisconsin, May 23, 1878	10,000
Portsmouth, North Carolina, July 28, 1880	90
Stanton County, Nebraska, September 29, 1881	1,000
Waterville, Kansas, May 30, 1879	300

In addition to these dry statistics, that government report quoted some vivid descriptions of those six hundred tornadoes. The second storm listed, one that struck Hancock County, Georgia, on the very warm afternoon of April 4, 1804, was presaged by a cloud front that "glimmered with a strange light." Soon the landscape was darkened by a black sky. Rains commenced and became a deluge. A funnel dropped from a cloud, although few persons would have seen it. Then, as some observer recorded, the "storm roared; darkness [was] intense."

Another random sampling of twelve entries provides these descriptions of tornadoes that once terrified Americans and no doubt remained for life in the memories of eyewitnesses:

Crawford County, Arkansas, November 8, 1879—The funnel interior appeared "as red as fire" to some fortunate person who saw it and survived. To others elsewhere, the "cloud looked like black smoke issuing from a large furnace."

Elkhart, Indiana, July 2, 1877—"Upper stratum of air greatly agitated; in lower stratum ash-colored clouds flew in all directions, converging to a common center; sulphurous smell in path of tornado."

Fort Lyon, Colorado, June 24, 1877—The funnel cloud "bounded along the ground and swayed from side to side."

Hartford County, Maryland, October 6, 1875—The funnel "formed a water-spout over Chesapeake bay; storm accompanied by roaring noise."

Hillsborough Pike, Tennessee, February 12, 1880—"Cloud bounded along over the ground; heavy blocks of stone, weighing tons, were thrown from walls of custom-house."

Holt County, Missouri, September 26, 1881—"Where the whirling cloud touched the ground the latter had the appearance of being washed."

Mount Carmel, Illinois, June 4, 1877—"Light objects were carried long distances—from one to fifty miles—and generally in a northeast direction."

Sangamon County, Illinois—"Fences running north and south thrown east and west; those running east and west thrown north and south."

Shelbyville, Tennessee, May 31, 1830—The central cloud "appeared double, having apparently two wings, like a large bird; they suddenly coalesced and came to the ground with great fury." The tornado that ensued carried a book "seven miles to the northeast."

Walterboro, South Carolina, April 16, 1879—"Balls of fire" were seen "dashing from the cloud. Terrible, roaring noise accompanied tornado; sixteen persons killed; fifty buildings demolished; loss of property $200,000."

Wellington, Minnesota, July 15, 1881—"Many animals killed, some of which had pieces of timber driven through their bodies."

West Point, New York, vicinity, July 13, 1875—An evening cloud that an observer could describe only as "large, black, peculiar," touched ground. "Trees torn up; teams and wagons blown over; very destructive."

"Very destructive" could describe almost any funnel that ever lowered itself earthward and became a genuine tornado for a considerable length of time. Usually applicable, too, is the adjective "capricious." Some freaks of past storms have become so common as to become clichés, and with one exception they won't be recounted in detail here: chickens bare of feathers that were apparently plucked by the tornado's vacuum-cleaning effect, straws and blades of grass blown into fence posts and left clinging there.

Some other freaks are not so commonly known. Consider these random examples, in addition to several happenings already mentioned—all authenticated by reliable men.

A tornado of extraordinary devastation struck St. Louis, Missouri, May 27, 1896, killing 306 persons and causing $12,904,000 damage. During the storm, one driver of a loaded wagon suddenly became aware of the absence of the team that had been pulling his vehicle. All animals, along with the wagon tongue, had been carried away by a wind estimated as high as 560 miles an hour.* Wagon and driver were left unscathed. Elsewhere in

---

* This guess, made by a Frank Bigelow, probably was too high, but the St. Louis tornado earned a reputation of having been one of the most violent to strike anywhere.

the city, people found a tree trunk with wheat straws embedded to a depth of one inch. On the following day, the 1896 Weather Bureau chief, Willis Moore, visited the scene of destruction and reported seeing those straws as well as these other sights: a 2×4-inch pine scantling driven completely through a piece of bridge iron more than half an inch thick; a gardener's spade stuck six inches deep into a tree, and a length of 6×8-inch timber driven four feet into hard ground. "Such was the fearful velocity of the wind as it gyrated about the small center of the tornado," Moore remarked in wonder.

Another tornado spun into Woodward, Oklahoma, near the Texas state line, on April 9, 1947, after having wrought a bit of freakishness substantially authenticated by Weather Bureau investigators. Near Higgins, in the Texas Panhandle, the storm roared in low over a residence. The owner, curious about the noise, opened his front door for a look and was carried upward, over treetops, while the unhinged door, also flying through the air, disappeared from his view. A male visitor in the home hurried to the same front entrance to see about his friend. The storm caught him, too, and sent him traveling upward, but on a slightly different course. Both men were lowered to the ground some two hundred feet from their takeoff point, suffering only minor injuries. They headed for the house, found the wind still too strong for walking, and crawled part of the way. At the residence site they discovered that the house had vanished except for the floor, a lamp, and a divan holding the owner's frantic but uninjured wife and two children.

Near Pryor, Oklahoma, a Red Cross worker en route to that town after a tornado had struck it on April 27, 1942, reported this bit of meteorological capriciousness. Every last board and nail of a small, square frame house had been blown away with the exception of the front porch, left standing without damage, and a wooden bench that apparently had been set leaning against the house before the storm. Near the porch was parked an automobile with a left wheel gone—blown away. But in the yard, under a large tree, stood a kerosene lamp, intact and burning.

During the disastrous tornadoes of April 3-4, 1974, that struck an area from Canada to the Deep South, winds pulled the insulation out of walls of residences and wrapped it around trees. The editor of the Cookeville (Tennessee) *Herald Citizen,* Charles Denning, reported, "It looks like a giant yellow and pink . . . cotton field."

One year later, another tornado created an odd scene on a Mississippi River expanse called Lake Pepin, which lies between Minnesota and Wisconsin. A storm struck that area on August 21, 1975, and sent lake craft of all descriptions flying about. One woman reported seeing houseboats sailing through the air above her own craft.

The very next year, still another tornado caught a woman driving a van west of Ogden, Illinois, lifted vehicle and driver into the air, and set both down in a cornfield half a mile away.

On June 17, 1940, a tornado whirled through central Soviet Russia, near the Volga River city of Gorki, picked up a treasure of coins laid bare by heavy rains that had scoured away the soil (said a Soviet observer), and scattered more than a thousand sixteenth-century kopecks around a small village. Those citizens then presumably worked frantically to become capitalists, although the Soviet observer didn't say so. Thirty-four years later, another tornado story concerning the same region filtered through the Iron Curtain, courtesy of the government newspaper *Izvestia.* In July 1974 it reported a number of deaths and injuries in Gorki caused by a tornado that swept a 100-yard path through the city, toppled three thousand trees, pushed a 240-ton crane into the river, ruined a sports stadium, and carried people and automobiles for some distance through the air.

Other freakish examples of what a tornado can do are as readily available as the nearest survivor who will talk about them. The monstrous winds have been known to lift heavy railroad cars vertically off their tracks, to transport an ice chest weighing eight hundred pounds for a distance of three miles, and to move a crate of eggs five hundred yards without cracking a shell. The most vivid imagination would be pressed to exceed or even equal tornadic reality, as a single story can demonstrate. Snowden D. Flora, a Weather Bureau meteorologist in Kansas for many years and author of a standard reference book (*Tornadoes of the*

United States), reported that during a tornado at Scottsbluff, Nebraska, on May 30, 1951, a bean was literally shot into an egg to a depth of one inch, where it was found embedded in the yolk. It entered with such smoothness, apparently, that it hadn't cracked any part of the shell around the hole.

Some sights a bit less freakish met my gaze as I entered the darkened outskirts of Waco that evening of May 11. An occasional frame house bulged weirdly and seemed on the verge of collapsing, with its bulk resting partly in the street or, in at least one instance, squatting in the center of an intersection. Scattered fallen trees almost as bare as defeathered chickens blocked sections of streets, while others remained standing where they had grown, still showing full foliage.

I had left U.S. 81 for downtown Waco at a location known locally as "the circle," somebody's early idea of a traffic engineering marvel, maybe, but in 1953 (and more so since then) a dangerous place where automobiles came together from several merging highways and sometimes crashed. After I had safely negotiated that obstacle and had taken a street that veered off to the left from U.S. 81, I neared the center of the city. The scene became increasingly grimmer. Encroaching night added starkness.

About the only friendly sight I recall now were some military personnel from James Connally Air Force Base, near Waco, who had been assigned traffic-directing duties—legally or not. A few men already carried flashlights, which soon became essential when the blackness of a cold, wet night gripped a city that had (as I soon learned) lost much of its electric power.

Even with the help of those airmen, I don't see how I managed to drive to, and park in front of, the Waco *Tribune-Herald*, near the downtown center and, coincidentally, near the area of greatest destruction.

I couldn't have gone any farther. Beyond my parking place, but mostly hidden now behind an evening veil not yet lifted by much emergency lighting, Franklin Avenue (which the newspaper plant faced) became a mass of clutter difficult even to walk over. Giant timbers, bricks, damaged or destroyed automobiles, some smashed flat, filled the street.

Change the names of the dying and dead and the survivors, touch up the times appropriately, and the scene I had more or less blundered upon might have been any one of numerous others created by violent tornadoes.

The National Oceanic and Atmospheric Administration has a list of the most destructive storms, beginning in 1925. The compilation, even though selective, is long and might be longer before this book appears in print. Here it is, with two exceptions. Information given for the 1974 tornado is based on my own research; and the 1953 Waco storm has been eliminated to avoid repetition.

DATE AND PLACE	DEATHS
March 18, 1925, Missouri, Illinois, and Indiana	689
November 25, 1926, Belleville to Portland, Arkansas	53
April 12, 1927, Rock Springs, Texas	74
May 9, 1927, Arkansas and Poplar Bluff, Missouri	92
September 29, 1927, St. Louis, Missouri	72
April 25, 1929, southeastern and central Georgia	40
May 6, 1930, Hill and Ellis counties, Texas	41
March 21, 1932, Alabama (series of storms)	268
April 5, 1936, Tupelo, Mississippi	216
April 6, 1936, Gainesville, Georgia	203
September 29, 1938, Charleston, South Carolina	32
March 16, 1942, central to northeastern Mississippi	75
April 27, 1942, Rogers and Mayes counties, Oklahoma	52
June 23, 1944, Ohio, Pennsylvania, West Virginia, and Maryland	150
April 12, 1945, Oklahoma and Arkansas	102
January 4, 1946, northeastern Texas	30
April 9, 1947, Texas, Oklahoma, and Kansas	169
March 19, 1948, Bunker Hill and Gillespie, Illinois	33
January 3, 1949, Louisiana and Arkansas	58
March 21, 1952, Arkansas, Missouri, and Tennessee (series of storms)	208
June 8, 1953, Flint to Lakeport, Michigan	116
June 9, 1953, Worcester and vicinity, Massachusetts	90
December 5, 1953, Vicksburg, Mississippi	38

May 25, 1955, Udall, Kansas — 80

May 20, 1957, Williamsburg, Kansas, to Ruskin Heights,
    Missouri — 48

June 4, 1958, northwestern Wisconsin — 30

February 10, 1959, St. Louis, Missouri — 21

May 5 and 6, 1960, southeastern Oklahoma and
    Arkansas — 30

April 11, 1965, Indiana, Illinois, Michigan, and Wisconsin — 271

March 3, 1966, Jackson, Mississippi — 57

March 3, 1966, elsewhere in Mississippi and in Alabama — 61

April 21, 1967, Illinois — 33

May 15, 1968, Arkansas — 34

January 23, 1969, Mississippi — 32

April 18, 1970, Texas Panhandle (series of storms) — 25

May 11, 1970, Lubbock, Texas, — 26

February 21, 1971, Mississippi Delta — 110

April 3 and 4, 1974, from Georgia to Canada — 350†
    particularly Alabama, Indiana, Kentucky, Ohio,
    Tennessee. (This includes the tornadoes that hit
    Brandenburg, Kentucky, and Xenia, Ohio, and other
    places on those dates.) A total of 148 tornadoes struck
    thirteen states during an 18-hour period, causing $1
    billion in property damage, 1,200 injuries, and the
    death toll stated at right. It was the worst tornado
    disaster in forty-nine years—since the 1925 tragedy
    that began this list.

The destruction I observed might have been seen in any of the above-listed localities on the dates given, or in many other victimized places not listed. The storm I'm writing about, however, is one that struck the center of Waco, Texas, on May 11, 1953. It was only one of 20,886 tornadoes recorded in the United States during the fifty-one-year period 1924–74—an annual average of about 410 such storms, which is a conservative figure now. The 114 deaths recorded in the city comprised only a fraction of the 10,943 persons killed by tornadoes from 1924 through 1974—an annual average of about 215. But in Waco, at least, residents still

† Some totals differ from this.

living who survived the dreadful afternoon of May 11 usually refer to that storm as *The Tornado*. That night and in days immediately following I came to appreciate the reason for this emphasis. Most of the rest of this story is theirs, and I have sought to let them tell it without much intrusion on my part.

6

A LEGEND OF SAFETY

Waco in 1953 was a small, nondescript, self-satisfied city of about 85,000 inhabitants who lived along or near the steep, brown banks of the Brazos River, a historic stream of greater dependability than most others in Texas and, with a length of 840 miles, the state's longest.

Early European explorers no doubt saw this river: La Salle, who apparently called it the Maligne, and Coronado, who (according to one story) named the river Brazos de Dios (Arms of God) after he and his men had been saved from the agony of thirsty deaths by Indians who guided them to its waters.

But those and other explorers would have come across the Brazos elsewhere. At the site of present Waco, for centuries before its modern founding, there had lived other Indians, amid the natural beauty and luxury of giant trees, abundant native grasses, and a plentiful supply of water, both from the Brazos and from a spring near the river that could still be seen gushing cool and clear in 1953.

The spring itself had been a main reason for the growth of an aboriginal population. The Indians, of a Wichita subtribe called Waco (better spelled Huaco and always pronounced WAH-co, although the city is WAY-co), were said to have had a superstitious veneration for the spring. As long as they could drink from it, they believed, they and their descendants would flourish.

Another belief attracted them to this location. Legend told them that here, on the banks of the Brazos near their spring, they would be safe from tornadoes and other violent storms that plagued inhabitants of the countryside around them.* The Waco City Directory for 1953 innocently elaborated: "It was traditional among [the Waco tribe] that the area was immune from the furies of the elements, for not in memory of man had there been a serious disturbance." When white men began flocking to the same Brazos banks about 1850, they heard the story and believed it. According to the legend, a surrounding rim of hills was responsible for ensuring safety.

For more than a decade into the twentieth century the saying proved valid. In 1913 a small windstorm destroyed a house within the city limits, at a location near Windsor Avenue and Twenty-fifth Street, but some persons denied this was a true tornado. The old legend of immunity remained alive for believers.

Genuine tornadoes struck elsewhere in the state: at Sherman, May 15, 1896, leaving 78 dead; Goliad, May 18, 1902, 114 dead; Tyler, August 21, 1918, 36 dead; Austin, twice on the same day, May 4, 1922, 12 dead; Amarillo, May 15, 1949, 6 dead. Even Zephyr, a community with a name that means "a gentle breeze," had a tornado—May 30, 1909, 28 dead. Few Wacoans worried.

Their city had been built in a picturesque area as well as a supposedly safe one—along the wooded Brazos banks. The river had dictated direction of the streets. Past the site of the city the Brazos flowed from northwest to southeast. Streets had been laid out parallel to it and numbered, beginning with First Street. In-

---

* At least one other community supposedly enjoyed similar security, until recently. According to another Indian legend, Spiro, Oklahoma, was safe from tornadoes because it lay between two rivers—the Poteau and the Arkansas. On March 26, 1976, a twister struck there, killing two persons and causing $964,000 damage in the vicinity.

tersecting streets running at right angles to First Street and to the river had been given names: Austin Avenue (the main street in 1953 and the one that divided numbered streets into "North" and "South" designations), Franklin, Mary, Jackson, Webster, and so on. Originally the "east" bank (as referred to locally, but actually north on a map) was mostly residential, the "west" (or south) bank commercial. By 1953, however, large residential areas for whites had mushroomed on the west side beyond the downtown section; blacks occupied much of the east side.

By that year, the dividing river had lost most of its scenic value. Municipal planners seemed blind to the beauty enhancement possible through such extra work as landscaping or simply cleaning riverbanks. Earlier, occasional Brazos floods had precluded extended development there, but by 1953 dams had fairly well controlled the danger.

So 1953 Waco sat on the banks of the Brazos without much effort to pretty itself. The most visible landmark around was a tall, thin skyscraper, the Amicable Building, which had had a reputation of being the tallest building in Texas for some years after its completion, in 1911. Its twenty-two stories poked 282 feet into the sky. When Artemas Roberts, founder of the Amicable Life Insurance Company, planned the skyscraper for erection four or five blocks from the west bank of the Brazos, he ordered it built to withstand any kind of punishment, including tornadoes. Into construction of the 20-thousand-ton building went 3,720,000 pounds of steel and 230,000 pounds of iron. Fellow businessmen reminded Roberts of the safety assured by that old legend, but they didn't impress him. The Indians, he replied, never erected a building stretching hundreds of feet into the blue yonder. For additional security and efficiency, he gave the building a generator to provide all electrical power needed, a steam-heating plant to assure winter warmth, and an internal water supply from an artesian well discovered during construction. In 1926 the Amicable offices commenced using outside electricity, but the generator stayed.

The building contributed to conversations of early travelers, maybe, but not to attractiveness of the place. During the first half of the twentieth century, white men's industry had hidden much of the natural beauty once enjoyed by Indians. The city could have been described as pretty only by people who lived in it and had learned to love it.

Nor did Waco seem very concerned about its future. "The city has a history of lost opportunities," said Professor J. W. Smith of Baylor University in 1952. Only a "minority faction" ever had been progressive.

He gave an example: In 1895 the city government refused to help the Santa Fe Railway build into Waco. As a result the town lost a chance for intensified trade development to accompany the founding and growth of a few other industries, including a soft-drink business named Dr. Pepper that originated in a building still standing near other railroad tracks. The local economy relied instead on cotton, and it celebrated this with an annual fair at a site called the Texas Cotton Palace. "Waco, geographically, was the center of the greatest cotton-producing territory in the world," Smith said. "In 1912 the twenty-one counties embracing a radius of seventy-five miles around Waco produced 27.5 per cent of the entire cotton crop of the state. Thus Waco took on the characteristics of an agricultural city and as such developed a rural ultraconservative outlook upon future growth."

The cotton economy plummeted, but the old outlook remained. More industry finally began to come during World War II, but lack of money still inhibited city development. Many streets were in exceedingly poor condition. The general futility seemed to come into focus in two locally renowned baseball anecdotes. Both involved a sharp-tongued local sports editor, Jinx Tucker, long dead now but a loud voice in 1953.

Late one baseball season, the oceanographer Jacques Piccard was reported ready to dive in his submersible (called a bathyscaph) with the aim of setting a new depth record. "I hope when he gets to the bottom," said Tucker, "he says hello to Red Barkley and his Waco Pirates."† On another occasion, Tucker

† That's the way the story goes, as I've heard it, and it would have been appropriate to 1952, when the Waco Pirates finished the season with a 29–118 record for the lowest percentage (.197) in all baseball. That left them fifty-six games behind the league champion. Authentication shows, however, that Tucker's remark would have come earlier, when the team was known as the Dons, not Pirates.

remarked of a Pirate pitcher: "He was knocked out in the third inning, but Manager Buddy Hancken didn't take him out till the seventh."

The struggling seat of government was two blocks toward the river from the "skyscraping" Amicable Building. There sat City Hall, in the middle of a square surrounded by a variety of run-down buildings, both frame and brick, housing butcher shops, dives that served beer only (in accordance with local law), pool-rooms, and flophouses. Off to the east, after the highway had been changed in the 1930s to spare long-distance motorists a trip through downtown traffic, most travelers were quite content to stare toward the city from a stretch of U.S. 81 and thank the state highway department for this fast detour around a remarkably unattractive locality. (Since then the scenery has changed, but that's part of the story to come later.)

Nor did the place show much of a personality then. What there was of one, seemed to be split. The city was once known simultaneously as "The Athens of Texas" (because of its educational institutions: Baylor University, Texas Christian University, now at Fort Worth, Paul Quinn College for blacks, Sacred Heart Academy, St. Basil's College, and still others), and as "Six-Shooter Junction" (because of frequent gunplay). Other cities have shown consistent character. New York long has had its bustling, everyone-at-his-own business attitude. San Antonio has become known for its Mexican flavor, which includes a Latin pride displayed in frequent bar fights and the ensuing casualties, and a Mexican casualness toward planning for tomorrow exhibited by city streets that now lead every which way. But Waco in 1953 was hard to place: a city without much apparent direction.

Since the nineteenth century and the start of classes at Baylor University, which operated under a different name then, it had become a stronghold of the sponsoring Southern Baptists. During the same period, its citizenry once included a Baptist-hater named William Cowper Brann, who built a worldwide circulation of 100,000 copies a month for his *Iconoclast*, published in Waco. Brann attacked not only hypocrisy, intolerance, and other evils he contended were church centered, but most violently of all, Baylor University—until a bullet fired on a downtown street on April 1, 1898, silenced him forever.‡

In those years and earlier ones, city fathers expressed pride in their many churches. They enforced laws against horse racing, Sunday opening of taverns and other businesses, and Sunday parades. But at the same time they legalized prostitution in a specified area through an ordinance dated July 12, 1871: "Every keeper of a bawdy house within the city shall pay an annual tax . . . of $200 for the privilege of keeping the same." Some influential and respected leaders claimed this was only being realistic: providing a section for sinning, thus keeping the rest of the city pure for the spotless. William Cowper Brann used another designation: "hypocritical." Nevertheless, the "Reservation," as it was called locally, remained open until World War I, when the U. S. Army forced its closing after establishing Camp MacArthur.

The personality split seemed noticeable even among local residents who became nationally known. From the supposedly conservative confines of Waco came Texas Guinan, whose real name was Mary Louise Cecilia Guinan, the daughter of a wholesale grocer. After attending Sacred Heart Academy, she left (before World War I) for a career in silent movies. During the years of national prohibition she became known in New York as a nightclub queen famous for the greeting "Hello, sucker!"

Even more sensational was the career of another onetime resident, Clyde Barrow, a dropout from Waco High School (and other schools elsewhere). While a student in Waco, he was arrested for theft of an automobile and given his first felony conviction. Later Bonnie Parker joined him for a bloody spree that included twelve murders, some kidnapings, and numerous armed robberies before their deaths, in 1934.

Less sensational and considerably more respectable was the career of Florence Gerald, daughter of a county judge, although her work, acting, couldn't be tolerated by "decent" nineteenth-century families of the locality. During her career she was praised by Alexander Woollcott, Heywood Broun, Channing Pollock, and Burns Mantle for dramatic performances that in-

‡ Some years later, H. L. Mencken read his prose and called him "a past master of invective."

cluded one with George Arliss. But when she visited her home town on tour, her father refused to allow her inside his house.

More than half a century later, another individual of artistic bent antagonized some citizens. In 1941, Madison A. Cooper, Jr., son of a wealthy grocer, began writing a novel that was published eleven years afterward, in two volumes, entitled *Sironia, Texas*. Its 840,000 words (on 1,731 pages) angered some residents, although Cooper claimed not to have been writing about Waco. The novel appeared on 1952 national best-seller lists for eleven weeks.

Other renowned residents have included two black men. This, too, is something of an irony, because in their days the city wasn't known for having any more racial tolerance than the area around it. One of the two men was baritone Julius Bledsoe, born in Waco in 1902. He later left medical school at Columbia University to study music in Chicago, Paris, and Rome before returning home to give his first concert, in New Hope Baptist Church. Later, under the professional name Jules Bledsoe, he appeared in the 1927 stage production of *Showboat*, where he sang "Old Man River," written especially for him by Jerome Kern.

The other black was Doris Miller, a 1939 dropout from then-Negro Moore High School. He enlisted as a navy steward, went aboard the battleship *West Virginia*, shot down four Japanese aircraft during the Pearl Harbor attack, and received the Navy Cross before meeting death aboard the aircraft carrier *Liscombe Bay* in 1943.*

The local personality split lapped over into one of status-quo maintenance versus progress. Founded on agriculture, the city displayed appropriate agrarian independence and conservatism throughout the years into 1950, as Baylor's J. W. Smith observed. Yet in 1911 that Amicable skyscraper, modern then if not beautiful, opened its doors, and local professional men deemed a business address there necessary for prestige. Even before that, some farsighted citizens had, in 1870, raised money to build a 475-foot suspension bridge across the Brazos, a difficult river to span then

---

* Still another seeming paradox regarding race came in the early 1970s, when a black man, Oscar DuConge, served as mayor with acknowledged distinction.

and a feat that brought commerce, travelers, and growth to the area. Two decades later (and prior to the 1903 Wright brothers' flight at Kitty Hawk), two men, named James Walker and W. D. Custead, working separately to develop their own flying machines, made considerable progress. Some area historians are fond of pointing out that Custead antedated the Wrights' triumph with a short, 1897 flight.

Further, local centers for child care were established at a time when many other Americans insisted that offspring should be the sole responsibility of their parents, all presumed to be loving and dutiful. A Methodist home for children opened in 1890, and an Evangelia day-care center began in 1907 serving children of women employed at a local wool mill. Both institutions still exist, with broader functions.

The split even lapped over into geography. Waco's McLennan County lay partly in a section known as the Black Prairie, to eastward, and partly in the Grand Prairie, to westward. Thus the city sat on a sort of east-west borderline, facing a sunrise that brightened "lovely rolling prairies [as an 1840 pioneer described it], swelling into high mounds, or stretching out in extended ridges of black, rich, sandy loam ready for the [plow] . . . and very productive"; and facing also a sunset that highlighted rolling hills, tall prairie grasses, and mottes of live oak and Spanish oak.

The east-west split seems to have had as much influence as any other factor, and it might even help to explain the apparent lack of direction prior to 1953. For years after its founding, the city was a true frontier town and showed plenty of western rambunctiousness. But it also attracted from the southeast a "respectable" and certainly a more refined social set. Many handsome antebellum houses built by those people have been preserved and may still be seen today. Considering the staid east and frontier west that went into the makeup, it is logical that there would have been a tug of war between respectability and rambunctiousness, conservatism and progressivism, independence and co-operation.

In 1953 Wacoans were musing over an American turn to the right. This move seemed especially appropriate for them and for their city, where conservatism predominated despite the occasional conflicts for two reasons: that agrarian background and the influence of Southern Baptists. Strangely but typically, however, local voters hadn't given the shift their majority support, further attesting to the difficulty of categorization.

Republican Dwight Eisenhower was in his first few months as President, but the county vote had favored liberal Democrat Adlai Stevenson by 16,913 to 14,621. This itself could have been a peculiar result of conservatism (meaning in this case preservation of what has been established), because the area, like the Old South, then had put itself in Democratic ranks traditionally and almost blindly. Further, the affection for the late Franklin Roosevelt and for his help to farmers during the Great Depression were still strong.

"Ike" had captured most of the rest of the state. The fact that Eisenhower was a native son had done much to persuade voters. Also influential were other factors: increasing weariness with the Democrats' concept of big government, begun under Roosevelt's New Deal bureaucracy, and an ensuing desire for a stronger local voice; lingering belief instilled by volatile Senator Joseph McCarthy of Wisconsin that Communists had infiltrated both the Roosevelt and the Truman administrations and were still slinking around Washington; and frustration over a peace that seemed continually to elude the nation that had won World War II. Not even five years had passed between the surrender of Japan and the outbreak of more fighting in the Far East—in Korea, where President Truman had ordered United States military units into combat against Communist North Korea, in June of 1950. On May 11, 1953, that "police action" still was in progress, at an eventual casualty toll of 157,530 Americans (including 33,629 men killed in action and 20,617 deaths from wounds and other causes). The conflict appeared increasingly senseless to Americans, especially since President Truman seemed to have avoided a showdown with Chinese Communists involved and had dismissed General Douglas MacArthur for advocating one. This resulted in Truman's having become the first United States President since Herbert Hoover to hear boos during a personal appearance.

In those years of Cold War tensions, Waco (despite its vote for Stevenson) and all America seemed quickly calmed by the election of the general who had led World War II allies across the English Channel to ultimate victory over Nazi Germany. This was true even though world dangers remained plentiful and obvious. Soviet Russia as well as the United States had exploded giant bombs capable of destroying entire cities. In November 1952 an American hydrogen-bomb test in the Marshall Islands had left an undersea canyon one mile long and 175 feet deep. Other nations were working toward capabilities similarly destructive. But with Eisenhower's inauguration, early in 1953, had come that greater feeling of security and serenity.† "Ike" intended to stop the war, and he had already met with considerable success in talking peace with North Korea. Then, in March 1953, the long-time Soviet dictator Joseph Stalin died, and though Americans doubted this would change the world situation very much, many of them were frankly relieved that the Soviet Government would be discomposed, if only momentarily.

Locally the new smugness expanded temporarily. At this very time in Waco it happened to include civil-defense preparations, but perhaps only coincidentally. In earlier years, when civil defense had been geared mainly toward procuring shelters for use in atomic attack, the city had gone ahead with a program but with little enthusiasm or understanding. Many residents believed that any superbombs would be aimed at fatter targets. Still, paper plans did exist, and one of them would figure in a grim irony before long. In event of nuclear attack it was presumed an enemy would aim at the block lying between Austin and Franklin avenues and between Fourth and Fifth streets—the most crowded part of downtown.

Eventually, other uses for civil defense would become obvious, but, that spring of 1953, most citizens still looked upon the proj-

---

† It wasn't to be a passing feeling, either. Twenty-three years later, after the administrations of Kennedy, Johnson, Nixon, and (to a lesser degree) Ford had occasionally rocked Americans in their boat, such a critical observer as Robert Sherrill of *The Nation* would remark (in the New York *Times Book Review* of January 18, 1976) that "as Presidents go, [Eisenhower was] the soul of stability and sanity."

ect with disinterest. A fairly well-equipped control center existed, but the city's first director had moved, and his staff had been disbanded. A second director had resigned after serving only a few weeks. The current civil-defense director, an insurance man, had been appointed on March 10, 1953, but he felt no urgency to complete his organization.

Nor did the mayor express any anxiety. He mirrored a local impression that modern warfare and civil defense were too complicated for common understanding. In his words, both were "too highfalutin" for most small cities to master, and Waco slid on toward its day of doom wondering when Baylor University would next win another Southwest Conference football championship to go with the crown it last captured in 1924.‡

Sliding seems a good word now to describe those times, but coasting might be better. World War II had given Americans an idea of invincibility that the Korean fighting hadn't really changed. A stalemate wasn't the American way of war and never would be. The American way led to total victory. The consequences of the development of atomic and hydrogen bombs hadn't yet been universally comprehended.

Further, the nation's economy was in good enough shape. The Korean conflict had helped it, although those comparatively few Americans still engaged in faraway combat probably didn't appreciate that fact. At home, many people had plenty of money, although salaries and prices were but a fraction of the level to which inflation would send them years later.

Local salaries were generally lower than those to be found in metropolitan areas nearby. Nevertheless, those were mostly good days, as anyone who lived through them probably would agree— especially now that he or she has aged by a quarter of a century. And if Waco wasn't the liveliest city around, at least life there could be comfortable and free from much of the stress that gripped more bustling and more prosperous localities.

For inexpensive entertainment there was radio—not yet usurped by a local television station, although an antenna could bring TV from Dallas or Fort Worth (and, on Sunday night,

‡ Success finally would come in 1974.

"Toast of the Town") into a properly equipped living room. But many listeners still dialed radios to Jack Benny on Sunday evenings from 6:00 to 6:30, and on the same night they heard Amos 'n' Andy, Edgar Bergen, Walter Winchell.

Sunday, May 10, 1953, had been Mother's Day. City churches were filled with dutiful daughters and sons of all ages, many escorting older women who were clearly mothers. That Sunday, the telephone and telegraph companies (as they reported later) enjoyed their greatest Mother's Day "of all time," and postal workers noticed the difference, too. Southwestern Bell Telephone handled 3,489 long-distance calls. Western Union sent and received a total of 6,000 telegrams. The Post Office delivered 1,482 special-delivery letters—more than four times the usual flow.

That evening, Lyndon Johnson, then Senate minority leader, addressed fellow Texans on a state-wide radio hookup, a weekly occurrence, but his subject wasn't mother. It was, instead, national security. "The greatest potential danger to our national existence," he said, "lies in the possibility of our becoming indifferent and complacent to such a degree that our nation could crumble from within."

Another hazard lying ahead surely escaped him that evening— or maybe Johnson meant to be including it. Ten o'clock radio newscasts later reported that two besieged French-Laotian outposts were still holding out against an angry surge of Vietminh Communists invading Laos. Area newspapers the next day also used the story, but not very prominently.*

On the following day a Waco mother returned to the forefront, but tragically so. Her son, daughter-in-law, and four young grandchildren were reported killed in a Sunday tornado that had struck near Hollandale, Minnesota.

Monday morning, the local newspaper carried a report of the distant tornado and the casualties, but without knowing that six

---

* Recently I looked again at page one of the Monday morning edition I, as telegraph editor, would have laid out Sunday night. I noticed under an unobtrusive, one-column headline "Vietminh Still/Attacking Two/Laotian Posts," a story datelined MANOI—a typographical error apparently never noticed and certainly not corrected. Years later it would be easy to remember how to spell Hanoi.

1. Cirrus clouds

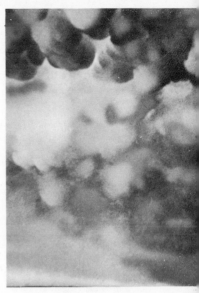

2. Mammatocumulus

3. Squall line clouds

4. Distant thunderstorm

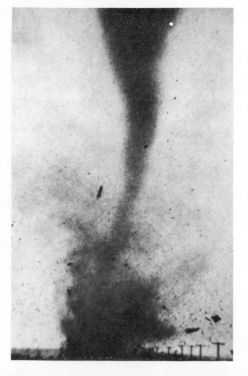

5. Organized rotary motion of a cloud (not to be mistaken for mere ragged edges) forewarns of danger.

6. When a funnel touches ground it becomes officially a tornado.

7. Prowler on the plains: a tornado near Elmwood, Nebraska, April 6, 1919.

8. One of the oldest tornado photographs: Miner County, South Dakota, August 28, 1884. Two secondary vortex clouds are visible.

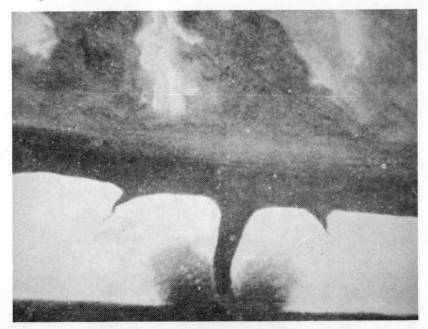

9. Waco damage. Old Tom Padgitt Building at right, Dennis Building ruins in center. Looking along Fifth Street toward Austin Avenue and Amicable Building, on corner at top left. (Jimmie Willis photo)

10. Franklin Avenue, Waco. Henson's Printing, Texas Seed, and Neely Paint companies were on the left side of the street. (Jimmie Willis photo)

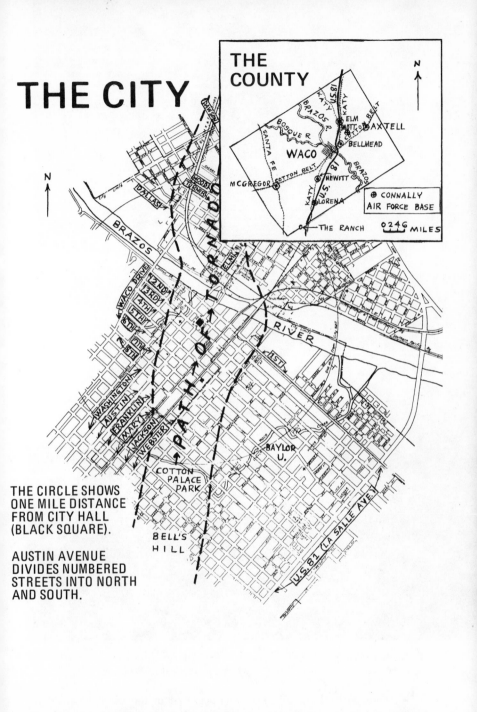

THE CITY

N

THE COUNTY

N

BRAZOS

WACO DRIVE

2ND
3RD
4TH
5TH
6TH

DALLAS

DALLAS

WOODED
TURNER

ELM

BRAZOS RIVER

1ST

WASHINGTON
AUSTIN
FRANKLIN
MARY
JACKSON
WEBSTER

PATH OF TORNADO

COTTON
PALACE
PARK

BAYLOR
U.

BELL'S
HILL

U.S. 81 (LA SALLE AVE.)

THE CIRCLE SHOWS
ONE MILE DISTANCE
FROM CITY HALL
(BLACK SQUARE).

AUSTIN AVENUE
DIVIDES NUMBERED
STREETS INTO NORTH
AND SOUTH.

In the county inset:

BOSQUE R.
KATY
BRAZOS R.
KATY
ELM
MOTT
AXTELL
BELLMEAD
SANTA FE
WACO
BRAZOS
COTTON BELT
MCGREGOR
HEWITT
U.S. 81
KATY
LORENA

⊕ CONNALLY
AIR FORCE BASE

THE RANCH   0 2 4 6 MILES

12. Cleaning up. Looking from old Padgitt Building ruins across Dennis wreckage along Fifth Street toward the Amicable Building.

13. Days later. Most of the deaths occurred in the block bounded by Fifth Street (at right), Franklin (cutting through the center of the picture), Fourth (to left, unseen), and Austin (unseen at the bottom). This was taken from the Amicable Building.

15. Brazos River, city in the distance

14. Austin Avenue today,
the Mall

17. Author, father, ranch
windmill, 1976

16. The *Brazos Queen*

victims were city residents. The afternoon edition rectified this with a lead story that ran under a six-column headline on page one:

SIX WACOANS AMONG DEAD
IN MIDWESTERN TORNADOES

Alongside the story appeared a picture of Mrs. Mary Vasquez, a 79-year-old widow, being comforted by a son, Joe. Mrs. Vasquez had just learned that the bodies of another son, his wife, and their children, who had gone to Minnesota as migrant farm workers eventually employed in asparagus fields, had been whisked from their flimsy tarpaper-and-clapboard house and blown seventy-five feet onto a road, where they had been found, battered and lifeless, early Sunday evening around the time when radio listeners were being regaled by Jack Benny.

A woman reporter visited Mrs. Vasquez Monday morning to write a story for that afternoon edition. The journalist found her subject to be a slight woman, shorter than five feet, wearing a black shawl that covered most of her gray head and hung limply across a pair of wilted shoulders. When Mrs. Vasquez could speak at all it was in a murmur. Her words were punctuated frequently with wails and with pleas for help impossible now to give.

The reporter returned to her newspaper and typed the story. "Almost unimaginable grief filled a dark little unpainted house in the . . . 900-block of South 1st Street today. . . ."

City residents would have been talking about that tragedy as Monday, May 11, progressed, although migrant farm families didn't attract much lasting interest. Residents also would have had these random news items from out of town for conversation stimulants:

A request by Senator Joe McCarthy, the Communist stalker, that advertisers boycott newspapers and magazines critical of him.

The British Mount Everest Expedition, led by Edmund Hillary, reported to be six thousand feet and an estimated ten days away from the summit.

President Eisenhower's new proposed budget, in which the

former general reduced the Democrats' suggestion for Defense Department funds by $5.2 billion, to a total of $36.1 billion.

The President's selection of Admiral Arthur Radford to be chairman of the Joint Chiefs of Staff.

Prime Minister Winston Churchill's suggestion from London for a conference of leading world powers to ease tensions: "It would be a mistake to assume that nothing can be settled with the Soviet Government unless or until everything is settled."

Roy Campanella's torrid hitting streak (.390) that had propelled the Brooklyn Dodgers into an early National League lead (with a 14–7 record), and Stan Musial's batting slump (.233) in St. Louis.

A heavyweight championship fight coming Friday night between Jersey Joe Walcott, who said he might retire afterward, and Rocky Marciano.

Locally, there were these happenings or coming events discussed that day:

A preinventory clearance sale, with "prices slashed as much as one-half" and with easy terms thereafter, at R. T. Dennis and Company, a large household-furnishings store standing across a street from the Amicable skyscraper.

A forthcoming week-long Home Show at the Heart o' Texas Coliseum, a huge building (a few miles southwest of downtown) large enough to seat eight or ten thousand spectators at Baylor basketball games, which didn't need that much accommodation then, and at rodeos.

Local observances of two other events: National Hospital Day on Tuesday, May 12, and Armed Forces Day on Thursday, when a military parade was scheduled for downtown.

A government economy move that endangered the local Weather Bureau office, which already had been trimmed from a forecaster and nine aides (in 1945–46) to a total of six employees. (Thirty-six stations elsewhere had been closed.) The abbreviated staff was responsible for putting a weather sequence on teletype every hour, twenty-four hours a day, seven days a week, said a reporter for the local newspaper, with the obvious hope that it might influence somebody somewhere to keep the office open. Further, the same newsman declared, local businesses had come to rely more on the Waco office for special warnings.

A continued scarcity of rain. Farmers, affected the most, talked about little else. Only those radio and television golden throats who read forecasts into microphones seemed to appreciate the endless days of sunshine.† At least one listener (as I well remember) once voiced an insane hope that sometime those announcers might turn on kitchen or bathroom faucets and discover their own water supply had dried up. In their continued favor, however, was the Monday forecast, as carried in Waco's morning newspaper: "Partly cloudy with mild temperatures today, tonight, and Tuesday. High today, 85; low, 55."

By afternoon, new weather developments had been recorded. That cold front, apparently ignored earlier by some forecasters, had begun to affect the western part of the state, although it was still miles toward a sunset from Waco. The same Monday afternoon edition that carried the banner story about Mrs. Vasquez and the Minnesota tornado victims also displayed a one-column headline on page one:

> STORMS HIT WEST
> TEXAS; 'NO CAUSE
> FOR ALARM' HERE

The story that followed included details of thunderstorms, scattered reports of tornadoes, and this paragraph:

> The Weather Bureau said thunderstorm activity would continue through Monday night. It said "there is a possibility of a few tornadoes in the [Texas] area bounded by San Angelo, Waco, Wichita Falls, and Big Spring."

That forecast had been prepared and put on teletype at 9:30 A.M. Central Standard Time by the New Orleans Weather Bureau after consultation with the Washington, D.C., office. Sev-

---

† This is repetition, but not exaggeration. The 1976–77 Texas Almanac has a sentence about the dry weather, on page 386: "The quarter-century since World War II was dominated by urban population growth and general prosperity in Texas, in spite of the longest [drought] on record, from 1950 through 1956."

eral meteorologists participated in the discussion, I have since
learned, including I. R. Tannehill, chief of the forecast and reports division. But the forecast was signed simply "[W. C.]
Conner, Weather Bureau."

Differences existed then among weathermen about the ad-
visability of predicting tornadoes. The Weather Bureau had been
issuing warnings since 1942, but the earliest ones were based
only on reports of individuals who had actually sighted funnels.
Advance predictions weren't attempted until 1952. Even then,
some officials believed that forecasts naming specific areas of
possible storms would only terrify people concerned and do
more harm than good. Another reason for caution was explained
by Francis W. Reichelderfer, chief of the Weather Bureau in
1953. "The Bureau occasionally gave out information [earlier]
that the weather map indicated tornadoes, but we felt that forecasts weren't accurate enough to publish as a definite feature
until [1952]."

The man in charge of the local office was a member of the old
school. He was kindly and thoughtful, as I was to see later while
interviewing him, and he was well liked for his humanity. He
sought to reassure people after other meteorologists had announced such a startling forecast, but he would regret that attempt until his death. The weather story also quoted him.

> In Waco, Weather Forecaster C. A. Anderson said
> there was no cause for alarm in Central Texas. Ander-
> son said at the time [1:30 P.M., May 11] that no tor-
> nadoes had developed in the area, and that if any did,
> they would travel over only a small area. He said they
> would be west of Waco if they did strike.
>
> He predicted strong winds, scattered thunderstorms,
> and probably some hail in limited areas.

The official forecast, carried in a page-one weather box that afternoon, was his, based on the second paragraph above, and
many concerned readers would indeed have been reassured by
it.

7

HOVERING OVERHEAD

That same Monday afternoon, the distant, high-banked cloud creeping in on Waco from the southwest again put weather into conversations of some persons who became aware of its approach. This was, of course, the same cloud my father and I had been watching. Area farmers who saw it would have reacted much the same way we had earlier. Their recently planted crops might have some chance yet instead of being doomed to die brittle deaths.

But the same sort of cloud had brought on a nightmare only hours earlier for a young housewife who lived with her husband and two-year-old son twenty-seven miles southeast of Waco, at a community named Lott. Mrs. Cecil Marion Parten, the wife of a sometime Baylor University ministerial student, had wakened crying from her dream. Later she elaborated on it. In her dream, she said, she had lost her husband somehow and was trying unsuccessfully to find him. All the while, a black cloud seemed to be hovering overhead.

Mr. Parten, twenty-nine, preached Sundays at the Lone Star Baptist Church in Lott. During this semester he was not enrolled at Baylor. Instead he was working weekdays as a bookkeeper at R. T. Dennis and Company, the large household-furnishings store across the street from that Amicable skyscraper. Pressure of work kept Mrs. Parten from relating the dream to him. She started to describe it, but he was in a rush to leave for the morning trip into town.

The ominousness of other clouds, these real, also left an impression on a local resident about midday that Monday. The clouds, however, weren't over Waco. They had appeared in skies over San Angelo, some two hundred miles west—the same city that had been mentioned with Waco, Wichita Falls, and Big Spring in the tornado forecast issued from New Orleans.

John Banta, a Waco newspaperman, had been called to San Angelo the week before because of his father's death. In early afternoon he and two brothers left their mother's residence in the northwestern section for downtown and some business regarding estate settlement. Once outside the house, they peered skyward and saw an unusual sight. "Look at those clouds," one of them remarked. "They're hanging down like bags." (Their scientific name is, appropriately, mammatocumulus.)

Banta's youngest brother, Bill, recently discharged from the Navy, said he remembered from an aerography textbook a picture of similar clouds. The text had stated that such formations have preceded some of the worst storms in history.

Later, from an office on an upper floor of a tall building in downtown San Angelo, they saw to west and northwest a dark cloud blanket covering the horizon. (All the while, but without the Bantas' knowledge, those state highway patrolmen had been following a disturbance already identified as a funnel cloud and had been making regular reports to their district headquarters in the city.) In time, after finishing their business, the three brothers took an elevator down to the first floor. A heavy rain shower forced them to wait inside for a while before leaving for their next destination, a social security office. There they learned that a tornado had ripped through the residential section known as Lake View. The same cold front that had helped spawn that twister raced on toward John Banta's Waco home, but again without his knowledge.

By midafternoon that day, which had become warm, muggy, and oppressive (as had the two preceding days), the horizon to the southwest of Waco had taken on its own ominous look. Even hopeful farmers would have realized by now that such weather wasn't bringing mere rain.

On a train called the Texas Special, nearing Waco from the south, George Tumlin, president of Dallas Marble and Granite Company, looked out a window and remarked to a fellow passenger that the giant cloud formation "spelled devilment" somewhere.

The Texas Special rumbled on toward Waco. At the "Katy" station, 801 Jackson, situated in a rundown area several blocks south of the center of town, the train gave a long, metallic scream and ground to a halt. Tumlin looked at his watch. Three fifty-five. He would have time to make a brief business call at Fifth Street and Austin Avenue. A cab could whisk him there and back in a very few minutes.

He stepped from his coach into a drizzle. Heavy clouds indicated more rain soon, but he walked to the depot, and to a waiting-room telephone, to call for an appointment—unsuccessfully, it developed, on such short notice. He boarded the train again and waited for its departure northward toward Dallas, his destination. Outside, the sky became darker still.

At Fifth and Austin, near the very office that Tumlin had hoped to visit, another Dallas man was working. Ira Baden, a slender-faced, spectacled employee of Nichols Engineering Company, had arrived in Waco earlier that afternoon with Roy Miller, company mechanical engineer, to complete installation of four sets of automatic doors in the Amicable Building. They had commenced the job during a visit ten days earlier and intended to finish it this time. While en route from Dallas they had seen clouds and had experienced wind so forbidding they had almost been persuaded to turn back.

Two of the heavy doors required trimming before they could

be put in place. Baden took them to the basement, where he was cutting them with a power saw at the very moment Tumlin, at the railroad depot a few blocks away, had been telephoning unsuccessfully for his appointment. Just before four o'clock, while Baden was working on his doors, building employees scheduled for the next shift began coming in to use their lockers, which were in the basement. Some early arrivals stood watching Baden operate the power saw.

Baden noticed building superintendent Louis Overton enter the room and heard him call for quiet. Baden stopped work momentarily while Overton, who had been on the same job for thirty-one years, told men of the oncoming shift about the Weather Bureau warning of possible thunderstorms and tornadoes, and instructed them on such safeguards as closing windows and vents. This would be no routine job. The 405 rooms in the building, which wasn't air-conditioned then, had 733 windows.

Baden and the superintendent exchanged a few words about the weather before Baden finished his work. Ten minutes later, Baden went upstairs to the ground-level entrance, where the doors were to be installed, and saw, outside, rain beginning to fall.

Half a block up Austin Avenue, Mrs. Margaret Charles had left The Fashion Shop, 413 Austin, for a coffee-break visit to Pipkin Drug No. 4, a block farther up the avenue, on the corner of Third and Austin, just across from City Hall. Ordinarily she took her break around two-thirty, but today she left an hour and a half late.

At the pharmacy, she remarked on the fearful afternoon darkness. Someone replied that a tornado warning had been issued. No one gave that subject much attention, Mrs. Charles remembered later, but she hurried back to her place of employment anyway.

Across the street from The Fashion Shop—and directly opposite the Amicable Building, where Ira Baden worked on the doors—stood a large corner building belonging to R. T. Dennis and Company, 426–28 Austin. This was where the Reverend Cecil Marion Parten was presently engaged in his bookkeeper's

job, having left Lott that morning before his wife could tell
him about her dream. Also working there, on the mezzanine of
the five-story building, was a gray-haired switchboard operator,
Miss Lillie Matkin, who had been employed in that job for
thirty-three years.

The weather outside would have been of little concern to Lillie
—the name by which she was known to the office staff—even if
she had been able to see it. Her immediate duty was to telephone
all department heads about a forthcoming conference called by
Dennis Company general manager Ed Berry.

Nor was the weather of any concern or knowledge to a mother
and her four-year-old daughter watching a double feature at a
movie theater on Austin Avenue next door to the Dennis Company. At the Joy Theater, 422 Austin, were playing two pictures,
Follow the Leader, with the East Side Kids, and *The Lusty Men,*
with Robert Mitchum and Susan Hayward. By four o'clock Mrs.
Jack Parnell and her daughter Jeannette had seen almost the entire show. Had they waited for Tuesday's matinee they would
have been offered something with a bit more regional interest:
The Lucky Texan, with John Wayne and Gabby Hayes, which
was scheduled to accompany *Here Comes the Groom,* starring
Bing Crosby and Jane Wyman. But a visit to a doctor's office
nearby had brought them downtown on this particular afternoon,
and they had decided to take in today's two features.

While Mrs. Parnell and her daughter sat through the last half
hour of their entertainment, a plumber worked on repairs in a
building just behind the theater. Lawrence Watkins, twenty-five,
an employee of W. B. Korioth Plumbing Company, was replacing a hot-and-cold-water mixing valve for the medical office of
Dr. Ernest Johnson. The office occupied space in a structure at
the corner of Fifth and Franklin called the old Tom Padgitt
Building, which stood to the rear of the theater and the Dennis
Company store—and was separated from both by an alley. (The
Dennis Company used most of this old building as a warehouse.)

The mixing valve had gone out two weeks earlier. Watkins'
company had ordered a new one immediately, but it had not arrived until that Monday morning. About 3:30 P.M., while the

Joy's double-feature performance was rolling toward a conclu-
sion, Watkins drove his truck into the alley between the theater
and the Padgitt Building and parked. He walked around the
corner and into Dr. Johnson's office, at 114 South Fifth. There he
encountered the doctor's assistant, Ted Lucenay, who showed
him how to get to the inoperative valve. Lucenay led him out of
the office, back around the corner, and to a side door opening
from the alley into the building. Through that door, Lucenay
said, it would be possible to go upstairs to the valve's location.

Watkins needed no other instruction. He found the valve and
took it out. The replacement, however, was of a larger size. To
make it serviceable he would have to fit on an additional piece of
threaded pipe. He walked outside to his truck, where he intended to prepare the piece, but rain forced him to bring his
equipment into the building.

Just across the street—Fifth—from Watkins, Harvey Claude
Horne, twelve, and his father were in the Hub Barber Shop, 109
South Fifth, watching the downpour. That morning, before
school, they had made plans for an afternoon visit to the shop,
and the low clouds that later had begun moving in hadn't de-
terred them. After Horne had paid for their haircuts, however,
they saw that the heavy shower would delay their departure.
They decided to wait for it to slacken before running for their
automobile, parked farther down the street.

Only a few doors from the Hornes, Mrs. Grady Goodman and
her 81-year-old mother, Mrs. J. M. Corbin, also watched the rain
impatiently, from a drugstore side entrance that opened onto
South Fifth. Mrs. Goodman had borrowed a car belonging to her
brother-in-law, Henry Dyer, and had brought her mother to a
doctor whose office was in the ten-story Professional Building, on
the corner of South Fifth and Franklin. The pharmacy, Williams
Drug No. 1, occupied part of the first floor and faced Franklin,
as did the building itself.

The women had been downtown since two o'clock. Mrs. Corbin's appointment with the doctor had ended shortly before four,
but by that time rain had begun falling so heavily, as they had
first seen from the lobby, that Mrs. Goodman suggested they
wait for a while to go to the car. For some time, they had

watched the shower from just inside the Franklin entrance to the
Professional Building. Then they had gone into the pharmacy
and to the side door opening to South Fifth, the street on which
Mrs. Goodman had parked. Still the rain kept them inside, the
same as it was doing to the Hornes in the Hub Barber Shop and
to plumber Watkins across the street in the old Tom Padgitt
Building.

Not far from the main entrance to that building, in a paint
store that adjoined it on Franklin, John Coates, twenty-six, had
heard about the possibility of a tornado. Aware of the darkening
day outside, he had begun to worry about the safety of his family: his pretty wife, Patsy, twenty-three, and two daughters:
blue-eyed, red-haired Sandy, five, and Kathy, born two weeks
ago. They lived in a white frame bungalow at 3904 Maple Avenue, in a residential area a few miles southwest of the center of
town, where Coates worked for his father- and mother-in-law,
Mr. and Mrs. Joe Neely, owners of the Neely Paint Company,
423 Franklin.

Coates dialed his home number. When his wife answered, he
mentioned the weather forecast of possible tornadoes.

"We're fine," Mrs. Coates replied. "It doesn't look bad out
here." She told him she was warming the baby's bottle with the
help of Sandy's five-year-old hands. She said when Kathy had
been fed she would call back with a list of grocery items for him
to pick up on the way home.

On up the same side of Franklin from the paint store, just beyond a bar and grill, stood the Texas Seed Company, 417
Franklin. There customers could buy pets and pet supplies as
well as a variety of seeds and other items from a pretty saleswoman, Dorothy McWilliams, and other employees. Soon after
John Coates had finished talking with his wife, three persons in
an automobile headed southeastward from a halt at Waco Drive
and Fifth Street. Their destination was Franklin Avenue and a
stop at that pet-supply store. Gloria Mae Dobrovolney, seventeen,
was driving. With her were her father, W. J. Dobrovolney, a civilian warehouse worker at James Connally Air Force Base
nearby, and her friend Barbara Johnson, a senior at Waco High
School. A parakeet at home needed more food, lowering clouds

notwithstanding, and the Texas Seed Company was the logical place to buy it.

Four blocks or so east of the seed company was a building housing the Brown Manufacturing Company, 217 Jackson—near the "Katy" tracks along which George Tumlin's passenger train was now gaining departure speed for Dallas. In the Brown Company building a woman employee who had seen tornado weather before was observing ominous similarities today. Shortly before 4 P.M., Mrs. Claude Pierce looked out at the blackening sky and remarked that it reminded her of some stormy weather remembered much too well from earlier days.

At a residence on Bell's Hill, an elevated area a mile or so south of the center of town, another woman who had seen tornadoes before—two of them—had a busy schedule of piano lessons to give that afternoon at her residence, 2209 Burnett. Mrs. Eugene Bullock, wife of a high school librarian, had just completed a thirty-minute session with young Bonnie Ruth Morgan, who had arrived at three-thirty. The girl stayed on while Mrs. Bullock began a four o'clock lesson with Dona Rozelle, because Bonnie Ruth was scheduled to practice a duet with a third girl, Myrl Wensel, after Dona had finished. Not long after Dona's lesson had begun, however, wind gusts began kicking around the neighborhood so alarmingly that Mrs. Bullock could scarcely concentrate on her work. Still, the last weather report she had heard discounted the possibility of another tornado entering her life today to go with the earlier pair—one in Kilgore, Texas, and the other in Arkansas.

In a cotton field outside the city a 65-year-old black man hired that morning with other hands to chop weeds found his work abruptly terminated. Pompey Dodson had been earning his pay with usual muscle and sweat while all that weather was building up to southwestward.

Typical of the time, Dodson wasn't really his own master. He chopped and watched the afternoon grow constantly gloomier, but when to quit work, or whether he should at all, wasn't really his decision. Finally, as Dodson said, "It got to looking so dark, the man [who hired the hands] brought us to the [City Hall square] and put us off there." By that time rain had begun to fall on the dumpy beer parlors and greasy-spoon cafes, pool halls, and flophouses that lined the block, and streets once dusty had become slick with a covering of mud.

Elsewhere around the city, thousands of others were on the verge of having their lives irrevocably marked or changed, although comparatively few realized the weather's portent.

At the Baylor University Library, on the corner of South Fifth and Speight, a student from Wisconsin peered out a window at the darkening sky and growing wind, and made a meteorological diagnosis based on his own experience. Andrew Oerke, a wiry, blond Golden Gloves boxer, had lived in South Dakota and Minnesota as well as Wisconsin, and in that part of the country he had seen many storms that were often called "cyclones" then. Some had been simply strong winds, but a few had been genuine tornadoes. Now another "cyclone" seemed to be prowling around nearby, Oerke reflected. Still, it didn't keep his mind completely off studies at hand. He was an English major, but he also had an interest in philosophy. One of his favorite professors happened to teach philosophy as well as English. That teacher, a man named Keith James, had just graded and returned to Oerke a paper on existentialism with a remark that it was the best undergraduate essay on the subject he had ever read.

About that time, the same Keith James and his wife were saying good-by to friends they had been visiting elsewhere in the city. James, who had earned a bachelor's degree from Wake Forest and a master's degree from Duke, had been teaching at Baylor for three years now. During the ensuing summer he expected to return to Duke to complete work on a doctor's degree. Having taken leave of their friends, the Jameses drove off with the intention of returning home—to 3724 North Twentieth Street. Their route would take them through the downtown area.

Also motoring along a street was Wiley Stem, assistant city attorney and commander of the local National Guard unit. He and several other occupants of a Parks and Recreation Department station wagon were on their way to do some photographing in connection with a lawsuit. Stem has forgotten details, but (as he told me recently) he still remembers a worry caused by the weather closing in: that it would make picture-taking impossible.

Recreation, not work, was the pursuit of some school-age boys that afternoon. At the Sun Pool, situated toward Bell's Hill in a park built on the site of the old fair called the Texas Cotton Palace, Billy Betros and other youths were swimming. Downtown, at Torrance Recreation Hall, which opened onto the alley that separated the Dennis and Padgitt buildings, a group of teenagers had gathered after school for a few games of pool. Among them were some members of the football team from La Vega High School, in suburban Bellmead, two miles northeast of the city. One of the youths was Kay Sharbutt, six-four and 260 pounds.

On the twentieth floor of the Amicable Building, Tenie Nixon, a young typist employed there, peered out a window that afforded an unobstructed view of the southwestern landscape and saw a storm approaching. The blackest part of it appeared to be coming from the direction of the 50,000-seat Baylor University football stadium, three miles or so almost due south of her. On another upper floor of the same building, the civil-defense director, Jim Meredith, also noticed the storm, while, far below him, Ira Baden worked on the doors.

Only a few yards from Baden, Bobbye Bishop, an employee of Williams Drug No. 3, 423 Austin, which occupied part of the Amicable ground floor, was looking forward to leaving work for the day, at four-thirty. But then her mother, who usually drove by to pick her up, telephoned to say that the weather looked so bad she intended to wait awhile before venturing out. Meanwhile, she said, Bobbye should wait in the store.

In a building next door, William Jess Garner also was completing his day's work: exterminating in the Thom McAn shoe store, 421 Austin.

Across the street, in the Dennis Company store where switchboard operator Lillie Matkin was now calling department heads to the conference, another employee, Bertha Mason DeGrate, whose daily hours were eight to four, found that her ride home would, like Bobbye Bishop's, be delayed by rain. She wanted to catch a city bus for East Waco, the black section of town across the Brazos River, but a downpour kept her inside. After waiting awhile, Mrs. DeGrate became increasingly restless. She walked to a back door opening onto that alley separating her store from the old Padgitt Building. Peering outside, she saw a continuing deluge. Shipping clerk George Conrad Roth, who had only minutes left to live, advised her not to go into the alley. Water cascading from drainpipes on either side could knock her down, he said.

Mrs. DeGrate then went to a side door opening onto South Fifth. Across that street was the Hub Barber Shop, where Harvey Claude Horne and his father had just finished getting haircuts. Rain and darkness almost hid the shop from view, however, and it did obscure her vision of the intersection, farther on, of Fifth and Austin.

But it was past time to go home. She decided to leave from the front door (opening onto Austin), walk up that avenue to Fourth Street, and wait there for her bus. As she was leaving she heard someone say, "I would wait awhile. You'll get wet." She answered that she had to go, then walked into the rain just as the Dennis nightwatchman, Tom Hurst, came in and unknowingly joined shipping clerk Roth and others for impending tragedy. Mrs. DeGrate walked quickly along a nearly empty sidewalk and got a soaking, but leaving the building when she did probably was the luckiest decision she ever made.

In the store Mrs. DeGrate left, business went on as usual, at least momentarily. On the first floor stood two employees, Beatrice Ramirez and Irene McCarty, both of them well aware now of the pouring rain. Not far away, Mrs. Carrie Patton, manager of the china and gift shop for more than thirty years, left her area for a few minutes to get a hat she had left in the women's rest room. On the mezzanine near where Lillie Matkin operated the switchboard, Mrs. Clara Faye Osborne worked at her desk. On the fifth (and top) floor, electrician Max Halve was repairing fans that would surely be needed soon, in the debilitating heat of another Texas summer.

For most persons inside, the expansive, lighted Dennis interior still hid the weather's portent. Elsewhere, however, more people were realizing this wasn't just another rain shower, even though few of them thought about a tornado.

City bus driver T. M. Hickman, making another run on his

North Fifth Street route, was approaching the Dennis Company building from northwestward, along Fifth. On the same street, but traveling from the opposite direction,* was Mrs. Earl Stinson, a Baylor University music teacher, driving a Dodge sedan through the deluge. Nearby, en route to pick up her husband, employed at the Professional Building, Mrs. Roy Temple drove a new Studebaker. She had planned to combine this trip with shopping, but the afternoon had become much too wet. And on a street leading to his residence a mile or so southwest, Harold Henry was heading home in a hurry from the Brazos Fish Market, which he operated on the east side of the City Hall square, better know locally as City Square. About four o'clock he had leaned over a counter too far and had split his trousers. He left the store, at 114 South Second, in charge of two employees while he went home to change.

In the industrial section near those railroad tracks running just south and east of the downtown area, Mr. and Mrs. W. C. Bowden, who managed the Lind Paper Company, 219–23 Jackson, had been working unaware of any storm clouds until salesman Wayne Darwin advised them to look outside. The weather seemed so bad, Mrs. Bowden said, "We decided to close and go home." Just next door, in the same Brown Manufacturing Company building where Mrs. Claude Pierce was thinking of tornadoes past and present, Mrs. Lynett Richards and others were about to leave work at the regular time. Mrs. Richards' husband was to pick up their children at school, then come by for her. She knew he would be waiting, rain or no rain, in front of the factory office on Jackson.

Three blocks away, Mrs. Rosa Porter worked with increasing nervousness on the third floor of J. M. Wood Manufacturing Company, makers of wearing apparel, 226 South Sixth—at the corner of Sixth and Mary. After lunch a young woman employee had brought back word of a tornado warning to Mrs. Porter, and as the hours passed and the sky darkened Mrs. Porter's anxiety affected her work. It was "probably not up to par," she admitted later. She couldn't stop looking out a window at the clouds, although her job called for inspection of cotton khaki pants coming

* Fifth Street is one way now but wasn't then.

off the factory line. On the floor just above, her son worked for the same company.

On a street in that industrial section, Edward Crook, a 31-year-old veteran of World War II infantry fighting, rode in an automobile with his parents, Mr. and Mrs. Lee Crook. He sat in the back seat, they in the front. Crook was no ordinary war veteran; he was a badly battered one. In Admiralty Islands fighting he had been hit in the left shoulder by shrapnel. After recovering and returning to duty he had suffered a bayonet wound in his right leg, during the battle for Manila. Those two injuries, in addition to malaria contracted during Pacific service, had weakened his once-rugged constitution. As an awful climax, after discharge in 1945 he had gone to work at the Veterans Administration Hospital in Waco and there had come down with tuberculosis, in August of 1949. For the following two years he had been a patient in another VA hospital nearby, at Temple. But even after release in 1951 he had been forced to return once a week for further treatment. Just seven days prior to this Monday afternoon—on May 4, 1953—doctors had pronounced him sufficiently recovered to return to work.

Downtown, in the Joy Theater, near where Mrs. Jack Parnell and her four-year-old daughter sat watching the last minutes of the double feature, Mrs. Susie Lain, seventy, heard a loud rumble that could only have been thunder from a giant cloud close by. Mrs. Lain had been in the theater since two o'clock and, like the Parnells, would be leaving in a matter of minutes.

A block down Austin Avenue, on the corner of Sixth Street, Ben Cocek and N. H. McGown, managers of the Walgreen Drugstore, 601 Austin, had been checking a store barometer since around four o'clock, when the afternoon began growing ominously dark. As the seconds ticked on toward the half hour, the instrument was registering 29.2. Five blocks west, on wide and fast Waco Drive, which provided a crosstown traffic flow from southwest to northeast, H. L. Linam was driving his automobile northeastward when he saw a familiar but frightening sight in the cloudy sky.

Linam was heading for home at Elm Mott, eight miles north of the city on U.S. 81. He had seen tornadoes before, and these

clouds had looked bad to him for quite a while now. Studying
the area of greatest density—off to his right—he saw what appeared to be a funnel that seemed to be moving on a course toward the downtown area and, if it continued, toward his own location. He stepped on the accelerator with the idea of
outrunning the turbulence.

Half a dozen blocks off to Linam's left, at the R. H. Brands
residence, 1225 North Fifth Street, the Brands' granddaughter,
LaRue Hagan, thirteen, was rolling up her hair with a young
girl's unconcern about life's vicissitudes. She had just arrived
home from school. "All of a sudden big balls of ice started hitting
against my window," she said. "I finished rolling my hair and got
me a funny-book to read." After that, she remembered later, "Everything was peaceful and quiet—except for the hail, of course."

8

APPROACH ON DOWNTOWN

So the same weather that had inflicted a tornado upon San Angelo earlier Monday had continued moving eastward, as fishermen and farmers from millennia past could have guessed in their own primitive way that it would.

The newest tornado had skipped through another community before hitting Hewitt, although I didn't know this until later that day. At Lorena, six or seven miles south of Hewitt, a local volunteer observer for the Weather Bureau, T. H. McBrayer, had gone to a hill west of the small town before four o'clock to watch the clouds approach. At 3:55 P.M. (as he later reported to Waco meteorologist C. A. Anderson) he felt a sharp breeze begin to blow. About 4:15 heavy rain sent him scurrying for shelter. Because of the darkness, he never did see a funnel cloud, but one had developed not far off, about the time the deluge began. At 4:10 P.M. the funnel had dipped down, officially become a tornado, and

destroyed the home of Mr. and Mrs. Wilson Stanford, three miles
north of Lorena. Furniture littered the yard. The Stanfords' refrigerator was blown fifty yards into a field.

After that, the tornado had struck Hewitt, at 4:20 P.M., with
the results already described. Just before 4:30 it was near the
southern limit of Waco, traveling on a course slightly east of
north—as countless similar storms had done. Until that time, the
funnel apparently had spent more time in the air than on the
ground, judging by damage done along its path. But at 4:30 the
funnel must have begun dropping earthward again. At that moment it was threatening an area between Baylor Stadium and the
hazardous traffic circle on U.S. 81.

Directly in the storm's path now stood the populated rise
known as Bell's Hill. Beyond lay the center of the city supposedly safe from such turbulence. Tornadoes had hit metropolitan areas earlier, of course, but never had one prowled into
the central section of a city as large as this one. Tragedy would
be written in the next few minutes, and much more swiftly than
this narrative can indicate.

The storm passed over Baylor Stadium during its approach on
downtown. In a stadium office at that very moment sat Mayor
Ralph Wolf, a vigorous man whose regular employment was
with the Baylor Athletic Department. Wolf was working at his
desk unaware of the extent of the lowering violence overhead.

From a point ten miles southwest of downtown, motorcycle
patrolman Al Blackwell of Waco saw the funnel. "It was . . .
narrow . . . but it got bigger and bigger, and I saw it dip
down. . . ." From a highway location eight miles east, T. E.
Caldwell, superintendent of schools at Thornton, in neighboring
Limestone County, saw the funnel and later described it: very
dark and apparently from one half to one mile wide. People returning from a burial at Rosemound Cemetery, in the southeastern section of the city, would have been aware of the ominous weather (even if they didn't see the funnel), but not the
Baylor University reference librarian seated at her desk advising
still another student which books to use for finding the information he sought, nor the doctor looking in on other patients at a
local hospital after losing one—a retired salesman—at 2:35 P.M.,

nor the janitor at an elementary school on the south side who had begun sweeping now-empty rooms.

But some observers watching from offices in tall buildings downtown had, of course, become aware of the storm's approach. To Tenie Nixon, the typist whose desk was on the twentieth floor of the Amicable Building, day seemed to turn into night. To Tom Street and H. S. Beard, attorneys whose offices were on the eighth floor of the Medical Arts Building, Ninth and Austin, the closing storm definitely looked tornadic. To Eugene W. Field, whose office was on the ninth floor of the ten-story Professional Building, something bad certainly seemed imminent. The clouds he could see about four-thirty were dropping rain in sheets and maybe some hail, too, in the vicinity of his own residence. He called his wife, who verified his fear. "It's hailing!" she said. "Big hailstones!" After he had hung up the telephone he looked around again—due south, in the direction of Bell's Hill and, farther on, the Baylor Stadium. Also in that direction, beyond the stadium, buildings of the expansive Veterans Administration Hospital should have been visible, but they weren't now. Moments later, the stadium also disappeared behind a curtain of rain and darkness. Above the stadium's location —or where Field guessed it was now—he saw a black, wedge-shaped cloud that moved quickly toward Bell's Hill.

About that time, a man whose office was on the same floor walked in to talk with Field about the weather. "Look at that!" exclaimed Tracy Sharp. "There's wind in that cloud!" They saw in the area of Bell's Hill, where Mrs. Eugene Bullock had been giving her piano lessons, trees "whipped about like grass" as that cloud of remarkable blackness moved closer.

A man riding with others in a truck traveling through the area that Field and Sharp were watching was experiencing the effect of the wind. In the 2300 block of Dutton, Roy Ledenham began noticing roofs flying through the air. A block or so farther on, in her residence at 2209 Burnett, Mrs. Bullock, the piano teacher, had been watching the same blowing trees that Field and Sharp had seen from a distance. Her apprehension increased as she saw from a window topmost branches across the street blown almost to the breaking point. Sometime around 4:15—fifteen minutes into Dona Rozelle's session—Mrs. Bullock had stopped the lessons. By that time the gusts had reached such force that she could no longer concentrate on music.

She soon had other problems, too. Driving rain sent water seeping under the back door onto her kitchen floor. She began mopping, but about that time Dona Rozelle's mother called to say that Dona should stay where she was until the rain slackened. Then Dona's father would pick her up.

Mrs. Bullock looked again at the treetops across the street and saw them waving even more violently. She "knew it was here." Pieces of lumber flew past her window. A wire alive with electricity fell across the doorstep. Boards blown from two houses behind hers battered the rear of her residence. Wind shattered a front window near the piano. Above the bathroom, a hole appeared in the roof, created by debris hurtling from neighboring residences.

Mrs. Bullock herded the girls into her bedroom and told them to squeeze under the bed, but low-hanging box springs prevented this. Despite the wind's roar they could hear the sounds of flying objects banging even more loudly against the house. "I said, 'Girls, let's pray. He's the only one that can help us now.'" Later Mrs. Bullock remembered that her young pupils remained commendably calm.

At another Bell's Hill residence, three blocks due east, four other persons were praying for their own deliverance. Mrs. Fred Stengel, Jr., wife of a policeman on duty downtown, had just closed windows and doors* of her house at 1008 South Nineteenth and had left with her two children to see about a next-door neighbor, Mrs. Ernest Collins, whom neighbors called "Maw." When blowing hail began pelting the house, Mrs. Stengel ran to the back door to see how her rabbits and chickens were faring in their back-yard hutches and coops, but darkness, rain, and hail obscured her vision. She could, however, hear clearly the "banging of things blowing about."

Then, looking around, she saw Mrs. Collins holding a hand over her heart in a gesture that implied she was having trouble breathing. Mrs. Stengel helped the woman into bed and told her children to sit in a space between the bed and the wall. "I talked

---

* Not a good idea for a tornado, but logical because of the rain.

to Maw to try to keep her mind off the storm," she said. Then she suggested they pray.

Several blocks north of Mrs. Collins' and Mrs. Stengel's residences lay Cotton Palace Park, with a headquarters structure at 601 South Thirteenth. On those grounds, at the Sun Pool, Billy Betros and the other swimmers had continued splashing around until the weather began to worry them and they got out. Wind commenced blowing at a fearful velocity, scattering trash cans. The manager, 18-year-old W. J. Strength, yelled from his small frame office near pool's edge instructions for lifeguards to grab the rolling cans. But then he realized the wind's speed and ran from the shack for the safety of a dressing room at one end of the pool. Above it towered a concrete wall left from the old Cotton Palace, a large building used years before during the agricultural exposition.

Three lifeguards followed the manager into a basement. Close by huddled the dripping swimmers, awaiting weather improvement. Instead of abating, however, the wind hit with incredible fury seconds after the four young men had reached the basement. The concrete wall crumbled on them all.

Six or seven blocks north of the Sun Pool, Buster Chatham and Jack Berger of the Waco Pirates baseball team had just left their office at fifty-year-old Katy Park, 700 Jackson, when wind carried away grandstand and office building.

At almost the same time, the blow was felt at Ninth and Franklin, where stood the building housing the daily newspaper, the *Tribune-Herald*, on the left-hand fringe of the tornado's path. Inside, the editorial staff had been working with the awareness that a noisy thunderstorm was moving in, but for them even those sounds were muffled. Outside, a printer who had just left the building realized the severity. Lecil Parker, Jr., had heard by telephone from his frightened wife that hailstones were pounding their residence across town westward from the newspaper plant. He determined to go home immediately, but he got only as far as the parking lot before being stopped. There he was sitting in his car when the tornado hit.

He saw hoods of automobiles parked in front of his own rise as if "some unseen hand was throwing them up." Through his windshield he saw pieces of roof and lumber swirling "in slow motion in a huge circle" in front of and above his vantage point. No doubt remained in his mind about what to call this storm. He rolled all windows down about an inch to avoid glass breakage.

Seconds later he noticed an empty green Chrysler roll from the parking lot into tracks of the Cotton Belt Railway, which paralleled Franklin Avenue one block to the east. Then he saw telephone poles standing along the tracks knocked down "like tenpins in a bowling alley." A pole came to rest on the Chrysler's hood.

On Cotton Belt grounds nearby, two railway employees had reacted mechanically to save themselves from the mighty whirlwind that began to kick around their vicinity so suddenly. O. R. Loving, yardmaster, had been sitting in his office only minutes earlier when he shouted to telegrapher B. R. Brownfield about the bad-looking clouds converging on them. "We walked to the big door entrance . . . and watched clouds and . . . trees blowing in the wind."

While they looked, an automobile carrying three women stopped just outside the door. One woman asked permission to remain there until the wind died. Within seconds the vehicle caught a violent gust and lunged as if in the hands of a fitful driver. Its occupants leaped out and ran into the depot.

On Bell's Hill, the turbulence moderated as the storm's peak passed on toward that Cotton Belt depot and on toward the center of the city—all in a matter of minutes or even seconds. Mrs. Stengel and her two children ventured out into the rain from Mrs. Collins' residence to check on the safety of their own home. It still stood, but with windows blown away and with doors open. Inside, water had soaked many furnishings. Mrs. Stengel seated her children at the kitchen table while she went into the back yard to see about the rabbits and chickens.

Boards, pieces of tin roofing, wires, and extra garbage cans littered the yard. The rabbit hutches were a scrambled mess, but no real damage had been done to life. Mrs. Stengel saw drenched animals scurrying about for shelter, but eventually she caught every rabbit.

Not far away, at the residence of the piano teacher, Mrs. Bullock and her young pupils found themselves safe though shaken by their ordeal, which seemed to have lasted much longer than the seconds that would have measured the worst of it.

At the Sun Pool, some youths dug themselves out of the debris, but others were entombed by the collapse of the concrete wall. Ironically, the frame office from which the pool manager had fled still stood, apparently undamaged.

Toward the downtown area, on the *Tribune-Herald* parking lot, printer Lecil Parker, Jr., noticed the great wind abate before his automobile had suffered real damage. Still, he worried about the situation at home. Parker drove around to the newspaper entrance, dashed through rain into the building, and dialed his residence. The telephone was inoperative. He ran back to the car and started the engine. He would still have to make the trip. (When he arrived home he would discover that his wife knew nothing about a tornado in the vicinity.)

A short distance east, at the Cotton Belt depot, yardmaster O. R. Loving and the three women had dived for cover when they finally realized a tornado was upon them. Telegrapher Brownfield also leaped for refuge, but Loving didn't see where. Part of the building caved in, but Loving never knew exactly when that happened and remained unaware of it until after the tornado had passed. Then he and the women emerged cautiously into a pile of lumber and bricks. Debris had buried the women's car.

Loving never learned their names. He didn't know when they left or where they went. When he saw his colleague Brownfield again, he noticed the man's face bleeding.

Then Loving heard calls for help from somewhere nearby. "I looked over to my right," Loving said, "and all I could see was the side of a face and an ear protruding from a pile of bricks." Carefully he dug into the debris and uncovered two men, who stretched and remarked they were unhurt.

At his Baylor Stadium office, Mayor Wolf was finishing the day's work while, downtown, the tornado began showing its violence. Wolf was preparing to leave for home, unaware that the mayoralty of so small a city could suddenly became demanding beyond measure, even for a man with a reputation for vigor.

9

"HERE IT COMES!"

A tornado veteran shopping with his wife at Penney's, in the 600 block of Austin Avenue, heard wind whine "like a power saw in a wet board." Chester Stockton, a painter who lived just north of the city limit, in Bellmead, knew from experience what that sound signified. He was a survivor of a May 6, 1930, tornado that struck Frost, Texas, and several other communities, killing forty-one persons and leaving $2,100,000 damage.

Now the weather was dogging Stockton again. Plate-glass display windows shattered before his eyes. Immediately thereafter he saw a man run into the store and heard him yell that falling debris had flattened an automobile with people in it.

In seconds the tornado moved on up Austin and several parallel streets. Only a few yards from Penney's and customer Chester Stockton, Walgreen's assistant manager, Ben Cocek, who had been watching the atmospheric pressure, ran over to his colleague McGown with the barometer in hand. "Look!" he said. "It's gone to the bottom!" At that moment, display windows shattered and fell.

Still farther up the street, in the Amicable Building, Tenie Nixon had long since given up all thought of typing at her desk on the twentieth floor. As the afternoon outside her window seemed to reach its darkest point, all lights went out. She felt the building sway slightly. "I ran down to the fourteenth floor in the dark and without stopping."

On the ground floor, the same power failure terrified Bobbye Bishop, whose work stint in Williams Drug No. 3 had just ended. But she had become frightened earlier, when hail commenced beating against the sidewalk outside.

After her mother had called to say she wouldn't be venturing out for a while to pick her up, Miss Bishop had impatiently telephoned a friend, Loyal Bloxam, a member of the Waco Pirates baseball team, and Bloxam had said he would drive by to get her and take her home. Bobbye had called her mother then to tell her this, but soon afterward had come the terror.

Seconds before the hail had begun to fall, Miss Bishop had spotted her friend waiting in his car, but the worsening weather had propelled her in the opposite direction: not out the front door to Bloxam's automobile, but to the back of the store, as far away as possible from the storm. When power failed, she was standing there, near a man and a woman and "a young dark-haired girl in a blue dress" who was sitting close to a pay telephone booth. "I hid my face in the girl's lap," Bobbye said. She heard but didn't see store windows suddenly disintegrate.

Shortly before that, Ira Baden, who had finished his work nearby, had walked out the pharmacy door holding a cup of coffee. The day had begun looking like "nightfall" to him, but, once outside, he could still discern thick clouds scudding across the blackened sky. He walked back into the store, placed his cup on a counter, and returned to the doorway. Wind began blowing in even greater gusts. His ears popped. "I felt lightheaded," he said.

He glanced at his newly installed doors, guaranteed as wind resistant, and noticed that one was ajar, inching outward. No wind was doing that, he realized. Extremely low pressure was responsible. Quickly he opened and braced the door.

Then his curiosity sent him venturing outside again. He heard a roar that grew increasingly louder until it became almost deafening. Nevertheless, he could hear that same sudden shattering of plate glass that came almost simultaneously with power failure and that terrified Bobbye Bishop. When that happened, Baden was standing at the outward end of a strongly anchored steel guide rail emplaced to divide the pedestrian traffic that ordinarily flocked in and out the automatic doors. To avoid being blown off his feet, he grasped the rail and crouched. Then he peered northward up Austin Avenue, the direction from which the wind blasts seemed to be coming at this moment. He saw a steel mailbox hurtle past, only inches from his head. In the street he noticed a parked automobile lurch forward several feet and ram a curb before stopping.

While he stared, more flying debris and wind-whipped rain seemed to blow with even greater fury. "I was conscious of trying to move back into the building," Baden said, "but I could not. The enormous pressure, plus the hypnotic terror of witnessing this unbelievable scene, kept me glued to the rail."

Inside buildings near where the awed Baden crouched, persons not previously frightened by the thought of a tornado suddenly had a variety of reasons for terror: outside blackness, crashing plate glass, power failure. Only a few yards northward, up Austin, and on the same side of the avenue, Mrs. Margaret Charles had become aware of this storm's fury only moments after returning to work in The Fashion Shop from her late and abbreviated coffee-break trip. Soon after her return, she noticed lights inside the store "pop" two or three times but without going out. Almost immediately afterward, a skylight shattered, sending broken glass flying around. Rain poured through the opening. Thoroughly frightened, she called to shop owner Max Chodorow, who was closing a back door. "Mr. Chodorow—"

"Oh, my God," he said. "Someone close the front door."

Fear had paralyzed Mrs. Charles, however, and she couldn't move. Nor could anyone else, as Chodorow soon saw. He dashed to the front door and closed it himself. The skylight was beyond hope.

Mrs. Charles stared outside. "It was black as night, and the wind was coming from toward City Hall"—the same direction Baden had observed it blowing at that moment. Another sight discernible soon afterward compounded her horror: a view outside of what seemed to be "boiling black smoke." She saw debris crush an automobile parked in front of the shop. Bits of the car flew away, carried down Austin Avenue by the wind.

"We all screamed. Mr. Chodorow said, 'There's nothing we can do but pray.' Then the lights went out and the front windows began to break and fly back into the store. We got as flat on the floor as we could. Everyone was praying. I talked to God face to face. I kept asking [Him] to take care of my mother and [my] little girl. . . ."

Across Austin Avenue, in a locally well-known restaurant named Chris's Cafe, Mrs. Mary Montgomery had been watching the weather with fascination equal to Mrs. Charles's, but without the same caution. She was standing near the front door when one of the owners, Angelo Sermas, shouted to her from somewhere toward the rear, "Come away from the glass! It's storming!" Mrs. Montgomery had retreated several steps when she saw and heard the building crumble. As in The Fashion Shop, across the street, everyone seemed to be screaming and praying at once.

In Torrance Recreation Hall, which opened onto the alley, a crowd of about twenty-five persons, including those La Vega High School athletes, were noisily engaged in entertaining themselves. Don Hansard of La Vega High was among a group of laughing, joking pool players who were oblivious of the sounds of weather outside. Hansard took careful aim and sank the "11" ball.

Back across the alley and next door to Chris's Cafe, between that restaurant and the Dennis Company building, stood the Joy Theater, whose projectors had been grinding through the double feature watched by Mrs. Parnell and her four-year-old daughter. Earlier, Mrs. Parnell had decided to leave, but when she and Jeannette walked to the lobby, she had seen rain blowing outside. They would have to wait awhile, Mrs. Parnell had concluded. She led her daughter back into the auditorium, to a location near the front. They were sitting there when power failed. The big screen faded into a black void that quickly engulfed everything. "Just a second later, I heard the walls begin to crumble," Mrs. Parnell said, ". . . and I heard someone holler to 'get down.'"

Only a few seats from the Parnells, Mrs. Susie Lain, the 70-year-old who had seen both features now, had just risen to leave. The thunder she had heard earlier had grown constantly louder. "As I started out into the lobby," she said later, "the lights went out, and everyone [began] running and screaming."

In the Dennis Company building next door, Beatrice Ramirez was standing near a wall adjacent to the theater when store lights flickered out, then went on again. She and Irene McCarty, still standing nearby, saw a company official, Rush Berry (Ed Berry's father), walk toward the front entrance just as a huge display window shattered. Bea Ramirez saw fragments fly past the man, but somehow they all missed him. Next she saw all the lights go out, this time permanently. Lightning flashes illuminated the figure of Mrs. Carrie Patton, returning from the women's rest room.

Mrs. Patton called out nervously. "I went to her and took her in my arms," Miss Ramirez said. "We both stood there while the lightning flashed, and we could see the last [front] window . . . break. We saw Rush Berry run toward . . . the side entrance leading to Fifth Street. That's the last I saw."

At her desk upstairs, Mrs. Clara Faye Osborne sat in darkness after the power failure and heard the sound of walls apparently cracking. She leaped under her desk and yelled for others to do the same. At the switchboard nearby, Lillie Matkin still worked the lines. "I heard somebody say, 'Here it comes!' And oh, such a crash of glass I never heard." On the top floor, Max Halve, the electrician who had been repairing fans, had begun walking down a stairway along a wall adjacent to the Joy Theater when the lights failed. "The top of the building was shaking like a sailboat in the wind, and it sounded like sledgehammers were popping away on the [lower part]."

Behind the Dennis store and across the alley, power failure left plumber Lawrence Watkins in darkness while he was working with the last union of that new mixing valve. He struck a match to light his way downstairs to his truck, where he intended to get a flashlight and complete the job. At the bottom of the stairs, however, he could see, outside, pieces of tin and other debris hurtling past. Then the building began shaking. Thoroughly frightened now, he began looking around for a place of safety. In the gloom he saw two steel beams and walked over to them.

Parked across Fifth Street from Watkins was Mrs. Grady Goodman. During a lull in the rain, she had left her 81-year-old mother inside the drugstore and had run for the automobile she had borrowed for the doctor's visit. Mrs. Goodman intended to drive the short distance down Fifth Street to the pharmacy side entrance and there pick up her mother. By the time Mrs. Goodman had seated herself in the car, however, another downpour had commenced. She started the engine, pulled out from the curb, eased around an automobile parked just ahead of hers, and came to a halt at the corner near where Franklin intersected Fifth. There she pulled up to the curb, in a parking space covered by the first meter on that side of Fifth Street.

Mrs. Goodman turned the ignition key to "off" and prepared to run inside the drugstore. She waved a signal for someone among a crowd of people peering out through a glass display window to hold the door open for her. At that moment, however, all the faces disappeared from her view. The silent watchers had retreated farther into the building, and Mrs. Goodman soon realized why. Even as she stared at the now-empty window, a bicycle and a huge sign smashed into the side door of the pharmacy, blocking her escape there.

Only yards away, Mrs. Roy Temple waited in her new Studebaker for her husband to leave for the day from the Professional Building. She had ceased worrying merely about what might happen to her car. Moments earlier, she had seen small pieces of debris tossing about and had thought, "Oh, my pretty car is going to get a dent." Then she realized the old Tom Padgitt Building was beginning to come apart. She had just wriggled from the driver's seat to the other side of the car when a building stone crashed into the vacated position.

Terror also had seized Mrs. Goodman. Peering around, she saw wires leading to a traffic signal at the Fifth-and-Franklin intersection twist and break. The signal crashed into the street.

Then she heard glass windows in the drugstore break "with a splitting sound" audible even over the roar. "Bricks, huge timbers, signs, and wire were flying by so fast I felt as if the car and I were actually flying in the wind." This debris was blowing down Fifth Street from the direction of the Amicable Building— apparent proof of a counterclockwise wind and a twister, if anybody needed it or cared now. "My first inclination was to get out of the car and run, but lucky for me, I was paralyzed with fear and could not move." So Mrs. Goodman sat there and mechanically pressed as hard as she could on the brake pedal, "to hold the car and keep it from tearing down Fifth Street." Despite that, she thought the car was moving, and she tried to dodge the Western Union office just across Franklin from where she had parked.

To Mrs. Goodman's left, up Franklin on the other side of the old Padgitt Building, were (in this order from her) the Neely Paint Company, where John Coates was now on the telephone ready to take the grocery list from his wife; a bar and grill; and the Texas Seed Company, where Gloria Mae Dobrovolney, her father, and Barbara Johnson had driven to buy parakeet seed. A few doors farther on stood Henson's Printing Company. Inside that establishment an employee who lived in the neighboring town of Gatesville was being reminded of earlier storms. Sam Edwards, a printer, had ridden out two typhoons off Okinawa while serving in the Navy during World War II.

About 4:35 P.M., a wicked flash of lightning had startled Edwards and other employees. This had been followed by a sound resembling a naval salvo. For two minutes thereafter, rain and hail poured from the skies, blown by high wind. Then came a comparative lull that impressed Edwards as being much too quiet: "a still, vaccum-like calm" that for a few seconds made him feel that his ears were bursting. Following that brief interval, he became aware of a window hurtling across the bindery room, and he heard a girl scream. He saw the building roof heave up and down "like a canvas top." He leaped for shelter between two heavy type cases and stayed crouched there.

Outside, on Franklin, Gloria Mae Dobrovolney and Barbara Johnson were in the front seat of their car completing the second of two circuits of the block. Miss Dobrovolney, the driver, had let her father out earlier at the Texas Seed Company those few doors toward Fifth from Henson's Printing. While Dobrovolney shopped for the parakeet, the girls would drive around the block, then pick him up. But as they completed their second trip the wind became so violent they stopped in front of the store.

Miss Dobrovolney saw her father standing near the entrance motioning them to come inside. Barbara Johnson jumped from the passenger seat and ran for the store. Miss Dobrovolney slid from under the wheel, toward the door from which her friend had fled—the car exit nearest the store entrance. She prepared to follow Barbara inside.

Two doors away, in the paint store next to the old Padgitt Building, John Coates was talking to his wife. The telephone had rung moments earlier. Mrs. Coates and five-year-old Sandy had finished feeding the newest arrival, two-week-old Kathy, and Mrs. Coates was calling to give her husband the promised grocery list.

Coates shouted, "Oh, my God, Patsy, the building's falling in."

At the white frame bungalow on Maple Avenue Mrs. Coates heard nothing more. The line had gone dead.

10

SCANT SECURITY

Persons who sought to ride out the storm in the scant security of automobiles had realized the true danger before others, huddled inside buildings.

Twelve-year-old Harvey Claude Horne and his father, after waiting inside the Hub Barber Shop, had taken advantage of a lull to run for their car, parked farther down Fifth alongside the Western Union office, 500–2 Franklin. They pulled out onto Fifth, crossed the Cotton Belt and Katy railroad tracks, then turned right onto Webster, heading for home, at 3404 Franklin.

After creeping ahead for four or five blocks, however, the elder Horne found his vision so obscured by rain and darkness that he pulled over to the side of the street and stopped, near a one-story brick-front building housing the Douglas Manufacturing Company, makers of mattresses and canvas products, 1001 Webster. Just then, young Horne saw things falling and flying.

At the same instant, he noticed that his ears began popping and that breathing became difficult.

At that moment, the car carrying Edward Crook, the twice-wounded infantry veteran of World War II, and his parents was traveling past the Douglas plant. Crook still rode in the back seat, his parents in front.

Inside the Douglas building, employees had formed a line leading to the front door, preparing to clock out for the day. Mrs. Claribel Shipley of the office staff stood first in line, with her card in hand. A few feet behind her waited shop foreman Brewer Anderson. Another man, L. T. Davis, stood about three feet from the front wall. Elsewhere in the building, some eighty other employees hurried to complete last-minute work before pouring into the street and scattering homeward.

A roar startled them all, and they saw the brick front tumble into the street. Wreckage buried "a passing automobile"* and crushed four other cars parked alongside the curb. Plant superintendent William Bredemeyer and a group of men hurried out as soon as they could to help the entrapped occupants.

One of the parked automobiles belonged to the Hornes. They had been staring through the gloom when they saw the front part of the Douglas plant tumble. Young Horne watched falling bricks crush an automobile nearby. Debris flattened half of their own car "to street level," but the front seat, which they occupied, remained intact.

When the front of the building fell, Edward Crook dropped to the back-seat floorboard. The automobile top above him caved in under the weight of all that debris. "I couldn't hear anything in the front seat," he said, "and I thought my folks had been killed." He called out for help, then began trying to extricate himself. He couldn't work his right leg free, and he was forced to stay where he was. (Later, after Douglas employees had freed him and his injured parents, doctors discovered that the twice-wounded former infantryman had suffered twenty-five bone breaks in his right leg.)

---

* The words quoted came from an eyewitness inside the building. The "passing automobile" surely would have been the one carrying Edward Crook and his parents, although the occupants weren't named (or known, probably) by the eyewitness.

Downtown, in the vicinity of the barber shop the Hornes had just left, other drivers were experiencing realities more appropriate to nightmares. T. M. Hickman, who had been driving his bus along Fifth Street before turning right onto Austin Avenue at a location diagonally across from the Dennis Company, covered another half block before realizing that this weather represented something more than a violent thunderstorm. Ahead he saw a yellow pickup truck flying through the air at a height of four or five feet, apparently about to hit him. He stomped on the brake pedal and halted the bus, avoiding a most unusual collision. Hickman watched as the airborne vehicle hit ground and came to a stop of its own. Within seconds a man leaped from it and ran into a building nearby.

Hickman kept his foot on the brake, but his bus began bucking "like a horse." His windshield shattered, but he could still see what appeared to be a woman's body blown from a store into the street. He was preparing to dash out and help her when he realized the "body" was a store mannequin. He drove on down Austin Avenue slowly, scarcely able to see anything at all.

At the intersection of Fifth and Austin, where Hickman had made his right turn only minutes earlier, Mrs. Earl Stinson, the Baylor University music teacher, would have just missed seeing the bus go by. She was sitting there in her Dodge sedan waiting for the traffic light to change. Off to her right, parked at a curb alongside the Dennis Building, another Baylor teacher waited with his wife. Keith James, the professor of English and philosophy, had reached Fifth and Austin en route home. At that point the weather apparently had become so bad that he had stopped to wait for better driving conditions.

Wind commenced battering Mrs. Stinson's car with fresh fury. "I knew there was nothing to do but pray, so I prayed," she said. Those scant yards away, the Jameses would have reacted similarly, and as the storm became even more terrifying they clung to each other. Debris from the Dennis Building fell on Mrs. Stinson's automobile, crushing all of it except for a section just above her head. A mountain of rubble buried the Jameses and crushed their car to a height of two feet, as workers would find eleven hours later. (They would also find the dead couple locked in each other's arms.)

Two or three blocks southeast stood the J. M. Wood Manufacturing Company. Inside, Mrs. Rosa Porter, inspector of newly
made cotton khaki pants, was fully aware that her nervousness
about the weather hadn't been without reason. Minutes before
the tornado struck, a maintenance worker had come to her third
floor to close all windows and shut off fans.

Then power failed, plunging the entire building into darkness.
Mrs. Porter groped toward stairs near the front. She stumbled
several times. Through a window, she could see, near some railroad tracks across the street, a wind-blown boxcar crash into two
automobiles.

Within seconds, the storm had rampaged through the rest of
that small industrial section. On a street near the Hubby-Reese
Company, wholesale grocers, 305-11 South Thirteenth, Mrs. J. B.
Craig and Mrs. A. J. O'Neal protected themselves and three children in the car by flattening the youngsters on seats and a floorboard and hovering over them. All the while, the women could
see flying past them sharp pieces of tin, 2×4 boards, glass, tree
limbs, and utility poles. Their car seemed about to blow away,
too, but it never did.

On the northern edge of the industrial district, Mr. and Mrs.
W. C. Bowden, who had closed the Lind Paper Company when
the weather began looking so bad, were trapped in their car just
outside the building. They had intended to drive home, but an
empty truck was blocking their exit. While they sat and waited,
the storm struck, instantly shattering their rear window. Then
roofing material from their own building began peppering the
car top. Mrs. Bowden opened the door on the passenger side and
was preparing to run for better shelter when a large piece of cor-
rugated metal slammed against the automobile. She stayed inside
and shut the door.

In the building housing the Brown Manufacturing Company,
adjacent to the north, Mrs. Claude Pierce had seen the day
darken steadily after her remark to other employees that the
clouds reminded her of tornado weather experienced in years
past. Finally she said she was leaving. Shortly before four-thirty
she ran downstairs to clock out, followed by three other women
workers she had promised to take to their bus stop.

Mrs. Pierce knew that a friend, Buddy Card, would be waiting outside to drive her home. From the building entrance, through a curtain of blowing rain and some hail, she saw him sitting in an automobile stopped in the middle of Jackson Avenue, facing Third Street. Other cars crowded the street, their drivers waiting for workers of the departing shift. Mrs. Pierce ran through the deluge and through ankle-deep water to the car, jumped inside, and shut the door. Card prepared to leave, but Mrs. Pierce asked him to wait for the other three.

At that moment, another Brown employee, Mrs. Lynett Richards, also was leaving work. Her husband had, as usual, first driven to school to get their children. Now they were all waiting for her in front of the plant, only a short distance from where Mrs. Pierce sat.

Mrs. Richards hurried through the elements and a flooded street to her automobile, while, only yards away, Mrs. Pierce's three passengers—Louise Plemons, Thelma Goss, and Betty Tadlock—made their own wet dash and settled into the back seat of the car driven by Buddy Card.

The delay made departure impossible. By that time, traffic had become jammed. Wind, lightning, and hail terrified them all. Mrs. Pierce cried and prayed. The back-seat passengers, she realized, were huddled as near the floorboard as they could get.

Mrs. Pierce tried to get out of the automobile, but when she opened the door the car seemed about to blow away. She managed to shut the door, but it flew open again. All the while, wind rocked the vehicle.

She saw the roof and one wall of the Waples-Platter Company building, 400 South Third, cave in on automobiles stopped in the street just ahead. "Most . . . had people in them." Then she saw a 2×4 board knife through the engine of one car. A plank crashed into the hood of her own.

Occupants of Mrs. Lynett Richards' automobile, only yards away, viewed the same horror. Mrs. Richards had reached the car and had just managed to slam the door against the wind when she saw the collapsing Waples-Platter building flatten automobiles parked nearby. Debris hurtled about. Timber, tin, bricks, and hailstones hit her own car, too, and constant pounding of the hail chipped off much of the paint. In the back seat her children screamed and cried and sought to climb into the front with her. She urged them to lie down where they were, but they were too frightened for that. Then she saw part of her own plant fall. She felt sure that if the rest came down it would cover their car.

Mrs. Pierce had seen the building collapse, too. "All . . . this time it was completely dark except for the streaks of lightning and the flash of electricity when wires broke." Still, she and the three women in the back seat could see the outline of the place they had just left. Louise Plemons was staring at it when she screamed, "There goes the factory!" A wall collapsed, and the roof fell in.†

No one else in the car said a word, but Mrs. Pierce covered her face and thought of friends now buried under debris.

Outside the Shear Coffee Company building, 319 South Fifth, a visitor from Florida, Mrs. Robert Russell, and her five-year-old nephew, David Frase, were trapped by other wreckage. They had been sitting in the front seat of an automobile when Mrs. Russell heard objects hitting it. Instantly she pushed David under the dashboard, then the rest of what proved to be a brick wall fell on them. Mrs. Russell realized they were both pinned in what seemed to be a tomb.

† The funnel apparently wasn't at ground level, since the automobiles weren't blown away.

11

"TORNADO!"

Downtown, many other persons were being buried dead or alive.

Ira Baden saw much of the destruction from his exposed vantage point—crouched near that Amicable Building guide rail, with an arm lock on it. He seemed unable to breathe, but his eyes functioned properly. He saw bricks hurtling past him almost horizontally—blown from somewhere northward, up Austin Avenue, he thought. Pieces of plate glass surely capable of dealing death flew past, too. Their whines reminded him of ricocheting bullets. His eyeglasses somehow stayed in place, providing protection against the wind and enabling him to watch tragedy unfold at split-second intervals.

In the direction of City Hall, he saw façades stripped from buildings. A structure adjacent to the Roosevelt Hotel, 400 Austin, lost roof and side walls. This gave Baden an unobstructed view of the interior. An office with desk, chairs, and filing cases lay intact but exposed. Beside the desk stood a man with his hat on "and an incredulous look on his face." Baden watched the man walk to the open edge of his office and glance downward, then turn and run toward a door that once had opened into a hall. The man turned the knob, stepped into space, and disappeared from Baden's view.

About that time, he saw someone else vanish before his eyes. A man ran out from the Amicable lobby. Baden yelled after him to come back, but the man shouted that he was going to see about his wife, in the Dennis Building, and he ran on into the street. There wind picked him up and whisked him somewhere. "He simply disappeared," Baden said. By that time "at least half a dozen" automobiles were rolling down Austin Avenue, "not on their wheels but sideways—top, side, wheels, side, top—as an oblong stone might roll downstream in a swift-moving current." Whenever the cars rolled to a stop, they gathered debris that began to look something like desert dunes.

Another building to northward apparently exploded, then fell. Baden saw wreckage from it hurtle in a sweeping curve toward building fronts directly across Austin from him.

In that area stood the Joy Theater, still advertising *The Lusty Men* on an intact marquee, but not for long. As Baden watched, that building, too, appeared to explode.* Its front pushed outward into the street and sank to ground level there. The roof fell across the area that would have been occupied by the movie audience, but it retained its arched shape and (as was learned later) caused surprisingly few casualties.

Almost simultaneously, Baden saw display windows in adjacent buildings, including the Dennis Company, shatter "as though clawed out by some giant mailed hand." He noticed the plate-glass front of Chris's Cafe break into fragments; inside, Mrs. Mary Montgomery would have been walking away from the

---

* Baden thus described the tornado as moving from north to south. Examination later by Weather Bureau officials showed without doubt the movement was from south to slightly east of north, as already indicated in this text. But Baden's story hasn't been changed. Further, by his own words everything seemed to happen at once and a firm judgment of time was extremely difficult.

window after Angelo Sermas' shouted warning. Along the avenue in front of these stores lay fallen power lines giving forth sputtering sounds like the repeated cracks of small-arms fire and an ensuing eruption of sparks that illuminated disaster.

A nightmarish series of vignettes recounted by various eyewitnesses who saw the tornado tear through various sections of the city helped to tell the story.

A mother and three children lay on their stomachs under a cotton mattress in the living room and waited for their home to blow away. The mother, Mrs. James B. Chapman, 623 South Tenth, felt that her eardrums would burst. She noticed the house twist, then saw doors fly open. The chimney fell, and part of the roof disappeared. They all "prayed aloud."

The owner of a blueprint shop stood near the front window of his store, 719 Washington, watching rain and hail. Ed Daniel didn't suspect a tornado until winds dropped in front of his store a large sign that apparently had previously identified a business situated at Twenty-sixth and Franklin, some twenty blocks away.

Eugene Ives was driving his pickup past the First Methodist Church, 403 South Fifth, when wind dismantled a steeple that towered above the building and sent it crashing to earth behind his truck.

Tom Street and H. S. Beard, the attorneys who had been watching the storm's progress from the eighth floor of the Medical Arts Building, 900 Austin, just missed seeing that. ". . . We looked out one minute and saw the spire of the First Methodist Church," Beard said, "and when we looked next it was gone." They also watched the storm rip off tin roofing of an automobile parking garage far below them, on Ninth Street. "See that blue car?" Street asked his friend when the automobile had been exposed. "That's mine." The two men stared as wind tore into more roofing and threw it into Street's car, ruining it.

Five blocks away, Eugene Field and Tracy Sharp had continued to watch the storm's progress as it moved from Bell's Hill toward the downtown section and their own vantage point, the ninth floor of the Professional Building. They saw tin and other debris flying through the air; then, when the tornado arrived, they heard windows of their building pop like firecrackers. The structure actually shook.

Diagonally across the street from the Professional Building, employees and customers at First Federal Savings and Loan, 426 Franklin, heard similar sounds announcing the tornado's arrival. They rushed inside the vault for protection.

Across Franklin and a short distance up the street, printer Sam Edwards, the survivor of two Pacific typhoons, knew the structure housing Henson's Printing Company wouldn't make it through this storm. Not far from him, another employee, Mrs. A. K. Williams, Jr., watched debris flying around, then realized the building was going to pieces. The second story dropped into Franklin and, with other wreckage, buried a number of automobiles there. Mrs. Williams heard a man's cry come from one of them. Sam Edwards and others rushed outside to rescue him as soon as they could.

Two blocks southwest, in the Southern Medical and Hospital Service offices, 112 South Sixth, "The lights went out; the wind struck; and we all dived for the floor," said an employee, Mrs. Roy Purczinsky. "Our building wasn't damaged . . . [but] . . . we could hear people screaming, crying, and praying outside in the street."

At Butler's Shoe Store, 511 Austin, an employee, Mrs. Homer D. Darby, heard nothing but roaring wind outside. She had waited on customers until the place emptied, about ten minutes before the tornado struck. Then she and other employees huddled in the rear of the store. When she looked out again, she was amazed to see buildings "lying flat."

At another shoe store, in the next block up Austin, William Jess Garner, who had just finished his exterminating job at Thom McAn, 421 Austin, dashed through hurtling debris with a seventy-five-pound exterminating machine strapped to his back but forgotten in all the excitement.

Walking along a sidewalk nearby, twelve-year-old Coy Miller of a neighboring town, Moody, realized that some incredible force had stripped him of all his clothes except for shoes and socks.

Farther up the street, attorney Woodie Zachry and others stared through a shattered window of the Roosevelt Hotel and saw across the flooded street a man's body. "Go help that man . . . !" they yelled over at a group of people peering out from another building. When no one moved, Zachry dashed out into the rain, soaking a new suit, and discovered that the "body" was a mannequin from a men's store.

Farther still up Austin, on the other side of City Hall, the two employees left in charge of the Brazos Fish Market by Harold Henry heard electric wires pop and short out as the tornado advanced upon them. Their employer hadn't returned from home and his change of trousers, and his store (in a building reputedly erected before the Civil War) seemed to be on the verge of blowing away. One employee, Emanuel Rubel, saw a blue car rolling over and over in the street outside. Only he and the City Hall nearby seemed steady, but for his own safety he crept under a 24×24-inch meat block. Walls and ceiling fell around him. Wind took part of his shirt. Beneath him, the floor thumped like "some monstrous engine." Around him, he heard people screaming. He and his co-worker survived, however—as did Henry, who finally returned and found his store a shambles.

Not so fortunate was an employee of the Appliance Service Center, 117 North Second—across the street from the market and on the other side of City Hall. Jerry Utley was killed there. A fellow worker, Eugene J. Lamb, saw the tragedy. "We were standing in the doorway facing Washington when [the tornado] struck with a whirling sound. Glass busted in our faces. We tried to get behind something for protection, but a big support column fell on Jerry before he could get away." Another man there, Floyd Simons, saw wind lift an automobile and set it down in a parking lot.

Near the tornado's path, a polio victim lay in a trailer-house bed chatting with her husband, "I could move my legs a little, but I couldn't stand on them," said Mrs. Mercedes Carbajal. She had been living in a relative's trailer home to avoid exposing her children to polio. Of them, the two eldest were living in the Carbajals' frame residence nearby, 601 Novelty, and the three youngest were staying with relatives elsewhere in town.

The storm's sudden roar sent Mr. Carbajal rushing outside to see what was happening. Mrs. Carbajal, who had been unable to walk without help, "jumped up and ran to the door" to look after the two children staying at home. "I tried to open it, but part of the house had blown against it and jammed it." Finally, her ten-year-old daughter, Nancy, opened the door from the outside. She and a brother had survived the storm, although the residence was wrecked. (The other three children lived through a similar ordeal.) After it was over, Mrs. Carbajal said, "I guess I'm still too scared to feel anything."

Outside the tornado's path, but not beyond its influence, two other polio victims, who depended on iron lungs to help them breathe, learned that power failure had stopped both mechanisms. For thirty minutes, until hospital power was restored, eighteen-year-old Braz Walker's iron lung was worked manually by nurses in Crippled Children's Hospital. Nine-year-old Jean Gentry was able to breathe for an hour without artificial assistance, and she made it through safely.

Downtown, the storm swirled on, and even in the remarkable darkness of that afternoon Ira Baden could see the funnel cloud tripping along above ground level but low enough to reach the buildings.† It looked like "a great, single-tipped auger, slightly tilted, the whirling tip gashing one spot and missing another as it moved along." In the square block bounded by Austin and Franklin avenues and by Fourth and Fifth streets, it missed very little indeed—and not much in blocks immediately adjacent.

One building certainly not missed was the Dennis Company store just across the street from Baden. The old structure hadn't been built reinforced with steel and concrete, although it had been designed to bear the heavy weight of several upper floors and the merchandise they would contain. Now twisting winds of incredible strength tore into a structural Achilles' heel. Baden saw the top four floors separate from the first, rise upward some distance, disintegrate, and fall at a tilt on ground-level debris. All this happened "in less time than it would take to snap your fingers." A mass of wreckage spilled onto the Joy Theater and the Torrance Recreation Hall nearby and into Fifth Street, alongside the building.

† Baden himself didn't describe the tornado as progressing above ground level exactly this way. This description is based also on a report made later, by W. C. Conner of the New Orleans Weather Bureau, after examination of the business district. Conner believed funnel height to have been from fifteen to twenty feet above ground level.

In the recreation hall, Don Hansard, after knocking the "11" ball into a pocket, had been laughing with others around him. For the past few minutes they had been hearing thunder, and they knew there must be a big storm in the vicinity. Then the roof fell in on them. "People were screaming and hollering and wanting everybody to help them," Hansard said. "I was screaming, too."

In the instant after Mrs. Jack Parnell had heard the Joy Theater walls begin to crumble, she had helped her young daughter under a seat. Then she had squeezed on top of Jeannette just as walls fell to the front and rear of their puny shelter. Mrs. Parnell closed her eyes and prayed. From the wreckage nearby she heard groans and screams.

Only seconds earlier, 70-year-old Mrs. Susie Lain, seated near the Parnells, had risen to leave the theater. She was walking up the aisle toward the lobby when the roof collapsed. A piece of lumber struck her head. Mortar peppered her. She could see nothing.

In buildings adjacent to the theater, other persons were suffering or were already beyond pain. Just to the north, in Chris's Cafe, Mrs. Mary Montgomery alternately screamed and prayed from her location under some buried counter stools. "I knew I fell near the coffee urns, where gas was burning. I was so afraid we would burn alive in all that horrible mess." Mrs. Montgomery heard later that none of the persons standing only a few feet from her, behind the counter, had survived.

On the other side of the theater, in the Dennis Building, scores were trapped, and many were dying or dead. But in first-floor ruins Beatrice Ramirez was alive. Fortunately for her, the floors above hadn't crashed flat but had settled in that peculiar tilt. Now she was buried under countless tons of wreckage, but she had some room to maneuver—even to stand, she soon realized, although she had to bend at the waist.

Beside her yet was Mrs. Carrie Patton. Bea Ramirez asked her companion if she was all right and heard the answer, "Yes." Then Miss Ramirez heard a call from someone nearby. Verba Jean Cook, another employee, was asking for help in working a leg free from something holding it. At that moment, however, a

scream from Mrs. Patton startled Miss Ramirez. Something had
her arm, Mrs. Patton shouted. In the darkness, neither woman
could see anything, but Miss Ramirez ran her hand along the
woman's body and realized Mrs. Patton's right arm was hanging
"by . . . a thread." Mrs. Patton herself said later, "I woke up in a
pool of blood and found my arm almost torn off. It hung by only
little fragments—cut to pieces [by] jagged pottery."

In mezzanine wreckage, Mrs. Clara Faye Osborne, who had
crouched under her desk when the building began to go, found
herself trapped, too. The entire floor had collapsed, but some
furniture cushions had fallen on her and had provided some protection. Not far away, Lillie Matkin, the veteran switchboard operator, lay conscious but motionless on her left side beneath
what proved to be fifteen feet of rubble. Both legs were doubled
up against her stomach. Heavy beams lay across her chest and
hips. "I could just wiggle my feet a little. I could hear . . . people talking. I kept screaming, 'Help, help!' But I couldn't get any
response, so I just started praying. I asked the Lord, if I couldn't
get out to take me then. I was ready."

Incredibly fortunate was Max Halve, the electrician who had
been repairing fans on the top floor. Moments after he had
begun walking down a stairway to leave, the steps started sinking beneath his feet. He seemed to be "floating on top of the
building with a ringside seat on the tornado." Something pressing against his body kept him in a vertical position.

"I didn't get to see much, because I was facing the east wall
all the way down. Suddenly everything stopped and I found myself standing hip deep in debris next to the Joy Theater wall, facing toward Austin Avenue. . . ."

Tornado oddities had saved his life. The roof above him had
blown off into Fifth Street, and the wall nearest him had slipped
groundward, beginning from the bottom. The entire experience
reminded him of youthful slides down slopes of a bluff. "I didn't
have time to get scared," he recalled years later. "I just slid."

Halve still had some distance to go when he stopped. He
found himself standing in rain on a pile of rubble twenty feet
high. His hands were free, so he dug himself out of the debris
and made his way down to street level. There he found shelter

from the downpour and remained for a while, taking personal inventory. Every tool he carried was still in his pocket. His clothes hadn't even been torn. He was still wearing his eyeglasses. Only his hat was missing. He brushed himself off. Just yards away, from inside the mountain of wreckage that had once been the Dennis Company, came groans and cries of less fortunate human beings.

Across the alley to the rear, plumber Lawrence Watkins was digging his way out of the old Tom Padgitt Building, now in ruins. He had just reached what he presumed to be the security of those two steel beams when ceiling and walls began to crumble. A brick struck his head. Lumber fell across his back. Something held his legs. He thought he was going to die, and he wondered what would become of his wife and three-year-old son.

More debris rained down. He covered his head with his hands. The deluge stopped just short of completely covering his face. He yelled for help. Then he found that his right arm was free to the elbow, and he began throwing bricks away from his face. Whenever he tossed one, however, others would be jarred loose and would fall around him. Finally he discovered a way to clear out the stuff. He noticed a hole nearby, and into it he carefully threw each brick. A few minutes later, he had worked the pile down sufficiently so that he could use both hands. Once, he stopped long enough to look around, and he saw a section of ceiling and some other heavy material leaning against those steel beams he had stood near for protection—wisely so, as he now realized.

Watkins thought he heard a shout. He listened, but heard nothing more. He wondered about the persons he had seen in Dr. Johnson's office only minutes earlier.

After working ten minutes more, he removed all the bricks from around his body, but he discovered that other wreckage was pinning his legs. More time and labor were required to get one leg free, then the other. Later, he remembered the moment as the happiest of his life. He climbed up the brick pile and through a small hole above him to the outside world, where rain was still falling. There he realized for the first time the extent of the destruction. He looked for his truck, but the pile of rubble made it impossible to see even the alley where he had parked.

Just across the street—Fifth—Mrs. Grady Goodman had seen the old Padgitt Building fall. Throughout the worst of the storm, she had sat in the automobile with her foot hard on the brake pedal, as if that could have any effect against this wind. The tornado caught and tossed about many automobiles on both Fifth and Franklin, as Mrs. Goodman had seen. They were blown "over and around and around like crazy." During the wind's peak, her own car pitched like an unbroken colt. It would rear up in the back, then plunge forward, then settle down again.

Despite her fear, Mrs. Goodman had managed to glance behind her, in the direction of the Amicable Building, and the skyscraper seemed to her to be leaning, on the verge of sending its twenty-plus stories crashing down on Fifth Street. "The wind was so full of water, bricks, planks, and everything else, the terrible roaring and blackness of everything, that I was practically scared to death. I never thought of getting to the bottom of the car, [but instead] sat in the middle of the front seat, straight up all during the storm. . . . My hands were clasped tightly in prayer, [but] the only words I remember uttering were 'Oh, God, please save us' over and over again. I seemed to hear my voice under the roar." It was while praying that she had seen the old Padgitt Building fall, along with others.

All buildings seemed to sink into the ground. ". . . My sensation was that I was sinking, too, and I did, into oblivion. When I opened my eyes next, everything was strangely still and I seemed to be in a trance. . . ."

Northward around the corner, on Franklin, John Coates and his in-laws, Mr. and Mrs. Joe Neely, and others lay buried in the wreckage of the Neely Paint Company. Just two doors farther north (or what had been recognizable as doors only minutes earlier), W. J. Dobrovolney, Barbara Johnson, saleswoman Dorothy McWilliams, and still others lay helpless or lifeless in the ruins of the Texas Seed Company.

Gloria Mae Dobrovolney had witnessed the entire tragedy. After seeing her father motioning from the doorway for her and Barbara Johnson to leave their automobile and come inside, Miss Dobrovolney had slid under the steering wheel and was preparing to run for the entrance—like Barbara, ahead of her. Seconds before she was ready to leap from her car, the building collapsed before her eyes. "I . . . saw Dad standing there by the door, waving for me to come in where I'd be safe, and then there were only falling bricks and mortar. Dad was under it all." Her friend Barbara was buried, too.

Some wreckage crushed the automobile, with Miss Dobrovolney still in it. As soon as the storm waned, however, a group of rescuers freed her. She ran, stumbled, and clambered across soaked debris to the rain-swept spot where she had last glimpsed her father. There she commenced digging into the wreckage until other rescuers pushed her aside, not realizing her purpose. Nor could they see the tears that streamed down her cheeks. Continuing rain had combined with countless tragedies to put that face on everybody around.

A few blocks northward, across the street from City Hall, Pompey Dodson, the cotton chopper whose Monday work had been cut short, found himself still alive. He had survived the tornado in one of the Negro cafes that lined the square.

The storm had struck his place of shelter immediately after demolishing the downtown area around Fifth and Austin, but not long enough afterward to make much difference on clocks. When the weather outside roared to its peak, Dodson flopped to the floor on his stomach. Even as he lay there, he said later, something told him, "Go see about your children"—two daughters and several grandchildren who resided in the black section, across the river. Dodson rose and saw the building fall around him, but he made a safe exit and saw automobiles outside "turning over and over." All around him, people began calling for help. He heard them, but he walked on toward home, 316 Tyler.

On the other side of town, bus driver T. M. Hickman was heading in the opposite direction. After averting a collision with the flying yellow pickup, he drove on down Austin in a slackening wind. But the rain still poured, and he could scarcely see. At Twelfth Street he stopped and hurried into a store for a glass of water. He remarked to bystanders that the downtown area had been hit by "a pretty good wind," then returned to the bus and finished his route. Not until he had completed the circuit and was approaching the vicinity of Fifth and Austin again did he realize how great a wind had struck.

On its way northward out of the city, the tornado roared into the black residential area, across the river. En route there it picked up, then dropped, the old Suspension Bridge. Some observers said the span rocked like a cradle, but it held.

The storm caught up with Bertha Mason DeGrate while she was riding a city bus that had just crossed a Brazos River bridge leading onto Elm Street. After leaving work at the Dennis Company downtown, she had caught the bus at Fourth and Austin, but before she had traveled a mile, the dark funnel had whirled overhead. Wind nearly stopped the bus. Mrs. DeGrate stared through a window at tree limbs, poles, and pieces of tin shooting through the air, while passengers around her screamed. Tar paper blown from somewhere began covering the windows. Mrs. DeGrate felt sure the bus would overturn, and she asked the driver to stop. He went on, staying in the middle of Elm Street and never taking his eyes off the road. Paper and other trash covered his windshield, but he peeped under and around it.

Off to Mrs. DeGrate's left, Turner Street Baptist Church was losing all its brick front. At East Waco Elementary School, 401–27 Turner, the storm took off most of the roof and the top floor, and left much of this debris in the next street farther on—Hood.

On that street, at 419 Hood, lived Mrs. Claude Johnson. She, her six-month-old daughter, her mother, and three of her sister's children were in the house when the tornado passed over the elementary school. Mrs. Johnson used her own body as a blanket to cover her daughter. House and chimney fell on them, but no one died.

Farther yet to Mrs. DeGrate's left, on wide and fast Waco Drive, which provided crosstown traffic flow, H. L. Linam had kept on trying to outrace the tornado he had seen just before it dipped into the downtown area. He sped across the river bridge en route to Elm Mott and home. A mile or so beyond the river, near the intersection of Waco Drive and Dawson Street, the twisting wind caught up with him after demolishing those houses and buildings around Turner and Hood streets. His automobile ceased its forward motion and began moving backward. He leaped from the car into a gusty blast and looked for something solid to grab. He noticed a plum tree nearby and tried to reach it, but he could make no progress standing upright. He flopped on wet earth and crawled and rolled to the tree. Once there, he clung to the trunk with both hands.

A house porch streaked past him. Wind began whipping him "up and down like a sheet on a clothesline" and almost blew him loose. Then the turbulence waned, and Linam knew he had survived.

He stood, looked around, and saw nothing at all. Moments later, he realized the reason for his blindness. He had lost his spectacles, and his eyes were covered with mud. He used rainwater to wash them, then found his glasses and his car—the latter useless now.

On the other side of the river, at her grandparents' residence, 1225 North Fifth Street, LaRue Hagan, the young schoolgirl who had rolled up her hair with vast unconcern about the weather, put down the comic book she had been reading. She heard a "rattling and knocking" on the back door, followed by a shout she recognized as coming from her grandfather, R. H. Brands. "Tornado!" he yelled.

LaRue ran to the door, then grabbed a coat. She, her sister, and her grandparents hurried over to the site of her grandfather's business—a trailer rental across the river, at 616 Dallas, just off Waco Drive. LaRue kept a horse there, sheltered in a barn erected on the property; she was worried about the animal.

A tornado surely had struck the place. LaRue saw trailers tumbled about and left in odd positions—even in trees. The barn had vanished, and hay littered the area. But she saw her horse standing on four good legs, just behind the rental office.

Pompey Dodson, bound homeward, walked across the Suspension Bridge after the wind had played with it. On the other side of the river he saw much destruction and flooded, cluttered streets.

"I don't know how I got home, but [soon] I was there," he said a few days later. "My house was full of water. I had to carry my wife out. Then she told me the one-legged man‡ was next door

‡ Not further identified by Dodson, who wrote of his experiences for the local newspaper soon afterward.

alone. I . . . carried him out. I guess the good Lord was with me all the way, because I found my children all safe, and the Red Cross helped us, and the one-legged man is still [sheltered] at Hines School."

12

"HELP ME!"

For minutes after the tornado swept on elsewhere, a deathly silence settled over the downtown area.

Wiley Stem, then assistant city attorney and local commander of the National Guard, remembers that eerie stillness to this day. The tornado had stopped his Parks and Recreation Department station wagon at Ninth and Austin during the return from picture-taking for that lawsuit.

Stem and his companions left the vehicle and walked toward City Hall, six blocks up littered Austin Avenue. The devastation reminded him of scenes from World War II, when he had served in the infantry. At one location he noticed an automobile picked up by wind and slammed down onto a parking meter, which could be seen poking through the top of the car. In some places he had to climb over steep hills of rubble.

City Hall he found to have been battered, too—but standing.

Windows had blown out, and rain had poured in. Stem's secretary told him she had crawled under her desk during the tornado. Then Stem heard policemen say that a number of bodies already had been discovered outside.

After that, he hurried over to the National Guard Armory, 523 Franklin. He found the building relatively undamaged and fifteen or twenty guardsmen already gathered there. No one had keys to "strong rooms," where the weapons were kept, but someone shot off the locks. Then Stem sent a detail of men to Texas Power and Light Company to get a generator. The armory soon had lights and radio communication, and not long afterward a first-aid station, a morgue, and facilities for mass feeding. Many guardsmen reported for duty without receiving an official call.

The state highway patrol, among the first to hear about the tornado (as I learned later), ordered district cars into Waco not long after receipt of a 4:37 P.M. report of wind damage to a house in the southwestern section. Seconds later, patrolmen heard of another house having been hit, but they never would have anticipated what followed. Nor did Nathan Solomon of A&A Ambulance. The first call came at 4:40 P.M., from Bell's Hill. Soon after that, city ambulance services were flooded with calls, but no one ever sent victims a bill for the help rendered.

In the Amicable Building, where he had watched the tornado's approach, Civil Defense Director Jim Meredith found a trunk line somehow intact and telephoned the Red Cross, Texas Power and Light Company (for two auxiliary generators), Lone Star Gas Company (to shut off gas mains), and other offices, including that of the state civil-defense co-ordinator. At the Southwestern Bell Telephone central office, downtown but just outside the wrecked area, the tornado had jammed switching equipment, and for a time no one there knew the reason. Within minutes, a man came pounding at the door shouting that buildings were caving in. Two company men, George Hutson and Justin Hoy, took a mobile telephone car through cluttered streets and helped to set up an emergency communications center in the devastated section. Other telephone-company employees worked frantically to relieve the jam.

But the city reacted slowly, for the most part. Immediate information about the disaster was hard to get. Earlier that afternoon, Tommy Turner, central Texas correspondent for the Dallas *Morning News*, had left his Professional Building office on a minor assignment. He had completed it and had returned to his residence, at 3821 Watt, when the telephone rang. An editor in Dallas was calling.

"What's happened in Waco?" the man asked.

"What do you mean?"

"Well, we hear you've had a tornado."

"Aw, nah. We've had some hail and high winds, but that's all."

"Well, maybe you'd better check on the rumor."

The tornado meanwhile had skipped on northeastward and had disappeared about five miles east of a community named Axtell. The length of its path measured twenty-three miles.

The storm left behind these other cold statistics: 114 dead, 1,097 injured who recovered, 2,000 automobiles demolished or damaged, 850 homes destroyed or partially wrecked, 196 buildings demolished or requiring demolition for safety, and 376 other buildings declared unsafe. Property damage totaled $51 million or more.

But those were impersonal facts. The human story was to be found in the debris, where people began trying to cope with problems unimagined only half an hour earlier.

Some persons couldn't cope right away. A man in a cashier's cage carefully restored an upset cash box, oblivious of ruins all around him. A girl in a store paid for a phonograph record and walked out through a display window devoid of glass. A pretty, red-haired woman, skirtless and barefoot in the rubble but wearing a fur stole, stared blankly at passersby and asked over and over, "Where did it go? Where can I find it?" A man who had lost all of his clothing with the exception of shoes and socks strolled along the street, apparently unaware of his nudity.

Others saw reality more quickly. Some male civilians immediately realized problems to be encountered by traffic, with all the lights out. They waded, coatless, into rainy, flooded streets still passable, to direct the flow of automobiles. Most immediately urgent, however, was the recovery of trapped survivors. Their cries could be heard by those who ventured outside after the wind's roar had given way to comparative silence. They were soon joined by others, who had learned of the tragedy somehow and had hurried downtown to help.

Andrew Oerke, the Baylor student from Wisconsin who earlier had suspected a "cyclone," left the university library and learned from someone that the downtown area lay in ruins. He and a group of friends hurried there, partly from curiosity and partly to help. When he saw the devastation, a compulsion to help outweighed any other consideration. "I went into a sort of condition of 'automatic pilot,' " he told me recently, "and left all feelings behind while we lifted bodies from the rubble."

In San Antonio, a thirty-year-old fire fighter who specialized in oil-field blazes heard about the tornado. Don Hill told his wife, "Honey, I'm going to Waco—maybe I can help." After arrival he extricated twenty-four bodies from debris, impressed everyone with his expertise in dealing with disaster, and stayed around later to establish a missing-persons bureau, with approval of city officials.

Rain continued to fall on the first rescuers. Of greater consequence, however, was the approach of night. With power still off downtown, that would certainly hinder rescue operations.

Some entombed victims were able to help themselves and others in various ways. A few dug to freedom. One was Beatrice Ramirez, trapped deep in the wreckage of the Dennis Building. She left the nearly armless Mrs. Patton long enough to try to help the other employee, Verba Jean Cook, free herself from debris. Perhaps the two of them could then assist Mrs. Patton.

Miss Ramirez began crawling toward the sound of Verba Jean Cook's voice. She squeezed upward through an opening and found the trapped woman. To reach the pinned leg, she had to hang head downward from a precarious position. The object holding Verba Jean's leg proved too heavy to move.

Another cry from Mrs. Patton pierced the darkness. "Help me!" she implored. "I'm bleeding to death!" Miss Ramirez wriggled back. Once more, she tried to work the woman's hand free of whatever was holding it, but again without success.

"Find someone to get us out of here," Mrs. Patton pleaded. Not far away, Verba Jean Cook was calling again for help. Miss

Ramirez crawled "in and out of small holes," fell into a freight-elevator shaft, and began climbing up a cable. She heard a man nearby crying for help, tried futilely to dig him free, climbed farther up the cable, and yelled for aid herself. Several men helped her from the wreckage. She told them the location of the three trapped victims.

After Miss Ramirez had walked clear of the Dennis ruins, bruised, cut, and bleeding, a man appeared with a bottle of whiskey. "You need a drink," he said. She answered, "No, thanks," but he and several other persons forced her to swallow some of the liquid. Then a woman standing nearby dug into her purse for pills. "Here, take these," she insisted. Beatrice Ramirez said, "They went down my throat while I was trying to say, 'No thanks.'"

The two women she had left behind continued yelling, to direct rescuers. Soon afterward, Mrs. Patton and Miss Cook saw flickers from flashlights piercing dark cracks. They were both freed. Mrs. Patton held her right arm to keep it from dropping to the ground. (Later the arm was amputated.)

Not far away, Mrs. Clara Faye Osborne, who had squeezed under her desk just before the mezzanine fell, used her fingernails to peck on a piece of tin—the only sound she was capable of making. Rescuers heard the noise and carefully dug her from the rubble, too. Irene McCarty, last seen by Beatrice Ramirez standing toward the front of the store, also survived, but with head and neck cuts.

A final death toll, however, would show twenty-two employees dead (including Dennis officials Rush and Ed Berry) and nine injured.

For two hours no one even heard the screams of switchboard operator Lillie Matkin. She was trapped fifteen feet below the top of the wreckage, and in its very center.

Next door, in the Joy Theater, rescuers reached Mrs. Parnell and Jeannette. Someone holding a flashlight led them from the ruins. Mrs. Parnell said, "I don't know whether I'll ever go to another show. . . ."

In the same theater, Mrs. Susie Lain, unable to see in the darkness, dug out from the mortar. She felt someone grasp her arm.

Clinging together, she and the other person struggled toward the lobby. When better light allowed Mrs. Lain to see her companion, she recognized her sister, Mrs. Arthur Jaynes.

In adjoining Chris's Cafe, Mrs. Mary Montgomery was still living—not crushed like those persons who had been standing behind the counter, and not roasted alive by burning gas from coffee urns. Across the street in The Fashion Shop, Mrs. Margaret Charles had survived, too. The tornado had left her dazed but not injured. She picked herself up from the floor and stared at the damage. Windows were gone. An assortment of strange objects had been blown into the store. Everything inside "was down and in a shambles." But Mrs. Charles located her purse, then told Max Chodorow she was leaving to see about her mother and her young daughter.

As soon as she walked outside, she saw, across Austin Avenue, the wreckage of Chris's Cafe, the Joy Theater, and the R. T. Dennis Building. "I stood there and watched them bring out a woman from Chris's Cafe, blood all over her, and I'm sure she was dead. Everyone was dazed." (The woman might have been the still-living Mrs. Montgomery.)

Mrs. Charles walked down Austin Avenue to the 1000 block "looking everyone in the face" and asking randomly about her mother and child. No one could answer the questions. With each passing minute, she became more frantic, but several times she was forced to stop and shake broken glass from her shoes. She searched vainly for taxis or buses for transportation home.

In the 1000 block she turned around and walked back toward the center of town. At Eighth and Austin she noticed a city bus and boarded it, but the driver told her he couldn't go anywhere "until the dead man was removed." She gaped and saw a body "all stretched out and dead." She left the bus (and after enduring more anxious moments finally found transportation and learned that her mother and her daughter were safe).

At the corner of Fifth and Franklin, Mrs. Grady Goodman had been left alive in the parked automobile. She noticed that a rear window had been broken and that the car frame had acquired numerous dents and scratches. Still, the automobile was in better shape than one just behind it. Wind had picked up that car, turned it over, and left it bottom side up on the sidewalk. Mrs. Goodman could see it lying there.

As soon as she regained control of herself, she got out, struggled through the side entrance to the Williams Drugstore, and called, "Mamma! Mamma!" She found her mother, uninjured, behind the prescription counter, where someone had led everyone in the store—as far away as possible from display windows.

Later Mrs. Goodman learned that her husband had survived the storm at Dunk's News Stand, only three and a half blocks distant on Franklin. Mr. Goodman and others cleared debris from the front of the car and used a wrecker to pull it free. They drove the car home and found it was "about as good as ever."

That happened much later. Immediately after the tornado, people who had survived it seemed disoriented and were acting as if bereft of their senses, or they were searching for friends or relatives, or they were clawing into rubble to rescue unknown victims whose muffled cries could be heard. Some other survivors sought simply to flee the area of destruction. Actions and their times of occurrence probably varied in relation to individual characteristics.

In the vicinity of the old Padgitt Building, an All-American football player from Baylor, Stanley Williams, and two others heard screams. They dug Mrs. Roy Temple out of her new Studebaker, now crushed. Mrs. Temple crawled out and at that moment happened to see her husband on the street searching for her.

Near the Shear Coffee Company building, a man heard five-year-old David Frase yelling—as his aunt, Mrs. Robert Russell, had asked. The man called others to help, and they freed the two from the wreckage of their automobile. Mrs. Russell's back had been broken.

Inside the Padgitt Building, Dr. Johnson's assistant, Ted Lucenay, who had shown plumber Watkins how to reach the mixing valve, was uncovered from debris with a broken left shoulder and with bruises and cuts covering his body. Also injured but alive were Dr. Johnson himself, secretary Mrs. Juanita Potts, and two women patients from the neighboring town of McGregor. Found dead was a registered nurse, Gussie Mayfield, who had worked for Dr. Johnson twenty-five years.

Behind the Padgitt Building, just off the now-cluttered alley, workers digging into Torrance Recreation Hall ruins saw the face and shoulders of Don Hansard, who had sunk that "11" ball. Surprisingly, Hansard could talk. A few other survivors lying beneath the wreckage made their presence known by calling out or by tapping on pool tables that had saved their lives. Rescuers piped oxygen into cracks leading to those depths.

In the same block, on Franklin, a policeman carried saleswoman Dorothy McWilliams from rubble that had once constituted the Texas Seed Company store. Injuries included severe ones to her face, which had been crushed. She was put in the back of an open pickup, there drenched by more rain, and taken to a hospital. Doctors at first believed her dead, but she had remained conscious the whole time. (Later a plastic surgeon donated his services and offered Mrs. McWilliams any face she wanted. She chose her own.)

At Cotton Palace Park, Sun Pool swimmers buried beneath the concrete wall were the object of rescuers. One of the missing boys was Billy Betros. His father, police Sergeant Eddie Betros, sought to keep traffic moving and to keep away the curious. Occasionally someone would ask him about the truth of a rumor that some of the swimmers had died. Betros would nod quietly without mentioning that one of the missing boys was his son. When rescuers found Billy, he was dead.

"Chaotic" best described the stricken areas as I was to see them after arriving in Waco later that evening. Two square miles of the city lay in ruins. In a section along Austin Avenue, only three buildings had been spared: the Amicable Building, the Roosevelt Hotel, and City Hall—but they had been damaged by wind and water. Those three structures towered over piles of debris and grim silhouettes of partially wrecked buildings. Rubble that covered streets and automobiles now blocked emergency vehicles. Power and telephone lines snaked through the ruins. Broken gas mains still threatened to add to difficulties already enormous. Rain continued to fall, but it proved beneficial at least by lessening the danger of fire. The few uniformed policemen on the spot sought, along with those civilian volunteers, to ease the traffic difficulties, but as time passed, the situation began to get out of control. When reinforcements came, they were heartily welcomed.

Other communications besides telephone service had been disrupted. The two radio stations went off the air and would stay off for two hours. Numerous suburban residents didn't know of the devastation. Some remained unaware of it until the following morning. Others, who had heard reports of it, walked outside their homes, saw the Amicable Building standing as always, and presumed the rumors of great damage to have been exaggerated.

Downtown, door installer Ira Baden was among the first of those who had begun digging for victims. As soon as waning wind allowed, he had stood up from the guide rail and peered around. He saw that the drugstore had lost every last piece of glass from its display window, but that the wind had left intact a number of wristwatches and jewelry pieces being shown for sale. Baden suggested to a store employee that these be removed quickly.

Next Baden noticed water swirling along Austin Avenue. It swept against piles of debris in the street and looked to him like ocean swells playing on so many islands. Sprinkled atop the rubble he saw a myriad of white dots: large hailstones melting slowly in the wet chill of this miserable afternoon.

From the drugstore entrance appeared Roy Miller, the company mechanical engineer who had traveled from Dallas with Baden. Miller, survivor of half a dozen tornadoes, apparently was still dazed by this one. "He must have been as confused as I," said Baden, who noticed that Miller took off his blue sports jacket and gave it for safekeeping to a stranger, a drugstore waitress. Then he saw Miller doff a new gray hat he was wearing. The man forced it down on Baden's head. "Here, look after these," Miller said, then waded across Austin Avenue and began digging into rubble. Baden saw the waitress, also disoriented momentarily, fold Miller's jacket carefully and place it in a refrigerator. Baden put Miller's hat on a counter and joined him in rescue work.

They and some other men began at Chris's Cafe, where they heard a man and a woman call for help. They dug out the man, then commenced clearing debris from around the woman. About that time, the first fire-department units arrived and took over that particular job. The firemen organized a cautious system: use of a human chain to transfer pieces of wreckage from the pile to the already cluttered street, thus avoiding further injury to the woman and to others buried beneath debris. Soon they brought out the woman, possibly the one Mrs. Charles saw and presumed dead. She was badly injured, but alive. Later Miller and others found the bodies of two of the three co-owners, Victor and Angelo Sermas.

Cries from the ruins of Chris's Cafe ceased after that. Baden and Miller clambered over wreckage to the Joy Theater, where people had been more fortunate. Baden saw the reason: that arched roof had held up. On the other side of the theater, however, the scene was incredible. There lay the Dennis Building, as if hit by a bomb.

Baden crawled into debris there. He saw a man's bare feet poking out from wreckage, felt for a pulse, found none, and went on toward what had been the rear of the structure, where he heard cries. There he and others dug out two men still alive but badly injured. While they were thus engaged, Baden saw a stocky man wearing overalls clamber out of the wreckage of the Torrance Recreation Hall nearby. "It's a miracle—a miracle," the man said in a daze. "Everybody dead in there but me—a miracle."

After that, Baden answered a call for help from some men in Franklin Avenue trying to dig into a smashed automobile said to have been carrying two persons. He helped clear away wreckage, then watched as the crushed body of a man was removed. He didn't wait to see the second victim taken out.

By the time Baden had returned to his starting point, the Amicable Building, within an hour after leaving it, National Guardsmen were patrolling streets, and personnel from James Connally Air Force Base, nearby, had come onto the scene. Military organization helped bring order—if only unofficially, because martial law hadn't been declared and never would be.

By nightfall, police had roped off devastated sections downtown and were holding back a crowd numbering into the thousands. Among them were people crying or praying for the safety of missing friends and relatives, others seeking unsuccessfully to volunteer help not needed now, and many who simply wanted a chance to gape.

A disaster-headquarters office was set up in the posh directors' room of the First National Bank, in the Amicable Building. This had more than central location for an advantage. Those provisions made by builder Artemas Roberts to make the Amicable self-sustaining quickly afforded headquarters workers their own power and water supply. After remaining for a time in City Hall, Mayor Ralph Wolf and aides moved into the headquarters there, along with civil-defense officials and military officers. For days thereafter, they worked long hours, taking a little time off for naps on couches or floors of adjoining rooms and for quick meals prepared in a mezzanine kitchen that belonged to the bank.

Wolf had learned about the tornado during a drive downtown from Baylor Stadium. His first reaction had been to suggest martial law as the best solution. The senior military officer in the city, Major General G. P. Disosway, of an air-force flight training command, disagreed. He urged civilian leaders to hold the reins. Wolf retained his leadership, but vast military assistance came after Governor Allan Shivers asked Fourth Army Headquarters at San Antonio for it.

Monday night, as my presence by then enabled me to see, floodlights operating on mobile power began to cut through the darkness. Ambulance sirens howled almost continuously. A steady thud of axes and picks gave forth a grim rhythm. A sound truck stationed in front of the Amicable Building blared orders to various individuals, units, and locations. The words were easily heard in the vicinity even above the clatter of equipment and the voices of rescuers. "There are people in there," came the admonition of Sheriff C. C. Maxey over the loudspeaker. He was urging quick but careful work in the wreckage of the Dennis Building. Sometimes there came reminders about not smoking. Those broken gas mains had filled the air with fumes. Later the amplification system boomed, "We have the Army and the Air Force in here now. We have plenty of help. Will all civilians not needed in the area please go home. . . . Too many people create a hazard. Please go home."

For many hours, workers brought out injured survivors. Eventually the cries ceased. After that, virtually everyone recovered was dead.

Among the last living victims rescued was Lillie Matkin, the Dennis switchboard operator who had been buried under fifteen feet of debris. Two hours had passed before anyone heard her cries for help, at 6:30 P.M. By that time, hundreds of men from James Connally Air Force Base had arrived, having been ordered into rescue operations by base commander Colonel Ralph Rodiecke. A group of airmen tried unsuccessfully to reach Miss Matkin by burrowing through debris from Fifth Street. Another crew began digging down into bricks, lumber, and other wreckage—carefully, because they knew any shift of debris could kill her.

By eleven o'clock that night, success seemed imminent—as a voice on the loudspeaker announced for the benefit of hundreds of workers who had heard about that unfolding drama. Still, rescue didn't come. Some newly uncovered obstacle always seemed to prevent it, although Miss Matkin was almost within reach.

Guards were posted to keep reporters and spectators away from the vicinity of the hole dug above her. Gas fumes permeated the wreckage. I learned later that Miss Matkin asked for oxygen and for ice to hold in her mouth. For hours, air-force Sergeant J. D. Smith of Bossier City, Louisiana, Airman 2/c Dennis Scholtz of Detroit, and others alternated in giving her oxygen, ice, and coffee, and in talking with her.

The coffee made her sick. She vomited "a white froth." But the talk seemed to help. Sometimes the airmen themselves would be almost overcome by gas fumes and would require oxygen.

At one time during the long night, rescuers accidentally dislodged a support and caused a heavy piece of wreckage to press harder against her. After that, Miss Matkin could breathe only with light, shallow intakes of air. But she could still talk.

Early Tuesday morning, still entrapped, she began to lose hope. A minister visited with her from atop the hole and bolstered her spirits. A short time later, new depression came. She complained of numbness in her legs. Rain had stopped, but the hours seemed to drag on so slowly toward sunrise.

Another air-force sergeant, Robert Spotts of Mankato, Minnesota, described the difficulty of freeing her. "At first [we thought] we could get to her from under two layers of floors, but the building kept sinking. We could hear . . . porcelain crack on the appliances, and we knew it was sinking. . . . Bulldozers working on the Austin Avenue side of the building were stopped at 2:30 A.M. because the . . . beam which held [her] was in danger of crushing her if any wrong pressure was applied."

More of Lillie Matkin's ordeal and the difficulty of the rescue work were indicated by a local reporter, Betty Dollins, who later climbed to the top of the Dennis ruins. I saved her story and have just reread it. From her vantage point she saw a mountain of bricks, mortar, and splintered wood that had spilled over into the alley to the rear. Each time someone else made the climb up, she said, the bricks settled a little more. Miss Dollins reported hearing occasional rumbles from far beneath her, and she could smell gas fumes. "From the top, the wreckage seemed to be a building turned inside out. Some . . . floors still had not caved in under the bricks. You could see through in some places. . . . Looking down from on top of the . . . wreckage, there were no streets visible. They were covered with water, bricks, planks, sand, heavy construction equipment, emergency power plants, ambulances, fire trucks." Once, a heel of her shoe caught in the bricks. An airman helped her free it.

Another local newsman, Woody Barron, crawled through a tunnel in the debris with some other men and described the view from below, in a clipping I also have. "We could smell gas escaping from broken mains. Water was running in torrents from broken pipes in the building. We could hear it gurgling through the piles of junk.

". . . [We] could hear . . . hundreds of rescue workers on top of the . . . debris, trying to dig their way through to victims they knew were underneath.

"We could also hear at least one trapped victim. It was either a cat mewing or someone whimpering in pain. . . . I couldn't tell . . . the direction [from which] the sound came. [But] we were helpless even to attempt to get to the . . . [sound]."

That described Lillie Matkin's situation on the night of May 11–12, 1953, when I left Waco for Temple, with notes and photographs, because of our deadline. Later I learned the outcome. About 5:30 A.M., after she had lain there in pain for thirteen hours, Sergeant Smith described her as calm. ". . . She asked us to make sure we got her shoes and that she wanted a steak dinner right away."

At 6:55 A.M. she was freed. Airmen carried her to a waiting ambulance. Dr. Aubrey Goodman, who had been standing by for this moment, gave her a sedative. Flashbulbs made a strangely silent display. They seemed to be lightning flashes, but without the thunder this time. Those pictures appeared in newspapers and magazines around the world, including the then-weekly *Life*.

Someone put Miss Matkin's shoes in the ambulance. The driver took her to Providence Hospital. There doctors found her injuries included a black eye, arm cuts, and chest, hip, and leg injuries, but they said she was suffering mostly from shock.

Not long after her removal from the Dennis Building ruins, power-driven shovels began scooping up debris and dumping it in trucks to be carried off. About midmorning, another downpour commenced, again soaking workers. By that time no more moans were coming from the wreckage. Anyone who would survive this tornado already had been taken somewhere for treatment.

May 12 had been set aside as Hospital Day in the city, and it truly became that. Ambulances had been in almost constant use since 4:40 P.M. the day before. They had been supplemented by a fleet of private cars displaying white cloths attached to radio antennas or to some other fixture. The injured they transported packed the two main hospitals, Hillcrest and Providence, and overflowed into James Connally Air Force Base and Veterans Administration facilities.

Admitting clerks at first tried to take victims' names, but they soon gave up that effort. Thereafter, for convenient and swift identification whenever possible, medical personnel taped to the forehead of each injured person (and sometimes a dead one) a strip of adhesive tape bearing name and address. When all rooms and beds filled, many injured were forced to wait in hospital corridors. There they sat or lay on floors or leaned against walls. Moans spoke wordlessly of their injuries. Around them walked persons who stared at their faces and their taped identifications, looking for relatives or friends. If that quest proved unsuccessful, as it usually did, the searchers would stop and query hospital personnel who appeared to be carrying lists of names.

After some preliminary confusion, the city's medical people, augmented by university premed students and other volunteers, performed superbly. Few of the injured who reached a hospital with a good breath of life left in them died thereafter. As a climax to this benefaction, physicians and surgeons of the McLennan County Medical Society voted that all treatment given tornado victims would be free. Members of the Waco Chiropractic Society voted similarly.

Downtown, the search for missing persons continued, but now they would surely be found dead. Earlier, at one o'clock Tuesday morning, the body of W. J. Dobrovolney had been uncovered beneath part of the Texas Seed Company building his daughter had seen fall on him. Four hours later, workers found the body of her friend Barbara Johnson.

That same morning, workers digging into Torrance Recreation Hall uncovered many bodies. Phil Hardberger, an eighteen-year-old Baylor student from O'Donnell, found two of them. One was a black attendant with his hand outstretched toward the body of a white teen-ager, who was still clutching the dime he had been about to pay for another game.

Fifteen others died in the recreation hall, including the La Vega High School giant, Kay Sharbutt. His six-four, 260-pound frame was discovered lying crushed at the bottom of the pile of debris by teammates who had survived the tornado. One of them, Ronnie Warnke, said, "He had his watch on, and his girl's ring was on one finger. We took the watch off. It had stopped at 4:45."

The search went on for days. On Wednesday a Waco reporter wrote, "Now and then another body would be uncovered in the downtown area and be taken to the funeral homes where those with relatives still missing waited anxiously."

Newsman John Banta, having returned to work after his tornado-marred visit to San Angelo, was assigned that beat. He still remembers vividly the lifeless bodies and the families who came to wait—some sitting together silently, some crying.

That same Wednesday, a crane operator working his machine in Dennis Building debris lifted a section of wall. Embedded in it were bodies of two women. Workers quickly covered the sight with blankets. Military personnel assigned the task of retrieving bodies were advised to try to do this job without looking directly at the victims. Ironically, other men digging in that same debris uncovered an unbroken 3×4-foot mirror.

On the following day, workers found in Dennis ruins the body of the Reverend Cecil Marion Parten. Mrs. Parten's nightmare had become reality.

For others, reality-turned-nightmare better described the situation. At the same time, however, that week in the city could be called a human triumph, in my estimation. People helped each other in countless ways (although there were the usual exceptions). Some persons worked such long hours they went to sleep on their feet—as did young John Boyett, who dug through ruins for thirty-six hours before someone noticed his exhaustion and sent him to a hospital. Cafeteria and restaurant people handed out hot coffee and food. Store owners contributed from their stocks (when available) blankets, gloves, flashlights, and other supplies. Contractors volunteered the use of heavy equipment. The Air Force and the Army sent more men and equipment from the base at Connally and from Fort Hood and Fort Wolters, celebrating May 14 as Armed Forces Day in ways unforeseen earlier. The Red Cross (which rushed $395,000 worth of aid) and the Salvation Army distributed food and clothing. Volunteers included boy scouts.

Mail deliveries to undamaged areas never ceased. Suburban banks quickly provided space and equipment for personnel from downtown banks to conduct business with their own customers. Even the Grim Reaper seemed to co-operate. For four days after the tornado, no natural deaths occurred in the city—something for which the city's embalmers, who were joined by twenty-four professionals from out of town, must have been thankful. But no help was available to the helpless Waco Pirates. Their scheduled

games had to be called off because of the absence of a grandstand. (Later, they moved to another town and completed the
season.) City schools remained closed for a week, but officials
were thankful that no student casualties had been recorded.

Before long, some survivors even found reasons to smile: another indication of human triumph. Signs left on three downtown buildings provided a little humor. Still prominently displayed on one store that had been stripped of virtually
everything inside were the words "Everything Must Go!" On another battered building was the announcement "Lost Our
Lease." And on still another store, now devoid of all plate-glass
windows, were the words "air conditioned."

National Guard Commander Stem, then a lieutenant colonel,
recently recalled for me another humorous story, although it left
him far from laughter at the time. A few days after the tornado,
he was showing Texas Adjutant General K. L. Berry around
town, with emphasis on guard activities. Berry, a retired officer
of the Regular Army and a veteran of the World War II Cor-
regidor battle, seemed impressed. During the tour, Stem drove
his general to a lot on Waco Drive where damaged automobiles
had been towed and parked temporarily. There they were met
by a sharp-looking enlisted man standing guard. His uniform
was spotless, Stem noticed with pride, and his rifle gleamed in
sunlight that had broken through clouds after days of rain. But
the man, as Stem learned soon enough, had been in the National
Guard only three days.

The soldier waved a friendly greeting to the two uniformed
officers. "How are y'all?" he asked. Lieutenant Colonel Stem became rather tight-lipped, but he saw that the general seemed to
smile. Stem drove around the lot, then came back by the guards-
man slowly, so that he would be sure this time to notice the im-
pressive brass in his midst and salute it. Instead the man
drawled, "Y'all come back any time. Glad to have you."

But the memories most citizens have of those mid-May days,
1953, are of a different kind. They remember the rescue work,
and the volunteer who stopped to say to a reporter, "You can't
get away from the smell of death. And you can't sleep for thinking of those poor people. So you just keep working." They

remember the death toll: 56 in the block lying between Austin and Franklin avenues and between Fourth and Fifth streets (which happened to have been the assumed aiming point of nuclear attack), 38 in the square around City Hall, 9 in automobiles, 5 in the area near the two railroads, 3 in residential areas, 2 in the 300 block of Austin, and 1 heart attack victim on a city bus (no doubt the dead man Mrs. Charles saw).

They remember suburban residents standing in small groups on lawns and in driveways in the gloom of Monday evening, May 11: people who had heard of the tornado and who were waiting hopefully for someone to return from downtown. They remember seeing amid the silent ruins of a poultry store near City Hall scores of chickens and two ducks pecking at bugs and at bits of sandwiches dropped by rescuers who had moved on to other debris. And at least one person, Baylor senior Fred Guffy, Jr., remembered (as he said later) a Negro man searching through wreckage in the demolished area of black cafes, taverns, and hotels near City Hall. The man was wearing a hat pulled far down over his forehead. In his right hand he held a golf club. With his left hand, he clutched a small green pillow that he used to wipe his eyes.

During those same days, Mrs. John Coates remembered her husband's last words from the Neely Paint Company before the line went dead: "The building's falling in." But even after learning of the widespread destruction, she expected him to come home; volunteers downtown were doing a remarkable job of digging out survivors.

Monday night passed without his return, and even without any word from him. Nor did she learn anything about the fate of her parents, who owned the store.

Tuesday came and went with more rain and with more long hours devoted to waiting. A cousin, Thomas Evans, told of the ordeal: "Patsy [Mrs. Coates] and Sandy have been at the front window almost constantly since [Monday afternoon] watching for John."

On Wednesday, another wet day, happiness seemed to have returned, but only for a moment. "A car with relatives who came from out of town to help pulled up to the house. . . . She thought it was John coming home. She ran out into the yard and collapsed in the rain. We took her and the baby . . . to the hospital."

When the body of John Coates was uncovered from debris that same day, nurses refrained from telling her, for a while. The next afternoon, Thursday, workers also found the bodies of her parents, Mr. and Mrs. Neely. They had died in each other's arms during that terrible afternoon when The Tornado swept through downtown Waco.

13

LATER

Twenty-three years to the day, and almost to the minute, after that stormy Monday, May 11, 1953, another dark cloud appeared off to the southwest of my father's ranch. This one wasn't of such an ominous hue, but it was large enough to mean trouble somewhere. Judging by its direction and course, that trouble could come in about the same locations as before.

But there were notable differences. One of them, I'd prefer not to mention. Both my father and I were twenty-three years younger in 1953.* Four- and five-year-old children whose experiences I have mentioned in the tornado story would now be twenty-seven and twenty-eight.

This time, the landscape around us looked more like Ireland than stereotyped Texas. Drought *had* returned for a time after

* My parents' deaths two months after this anniversary date have been mentioned in a Chapter 1 footnote.

the 1953 tornado, but that was years ago. In 1976 a wet spring
had left farmers complaining and hurting, as most seasons seem
to leave them. It's not that farmers really want to complain—
simply that the various hazards of their livelihood frequently
move them in that direction.

But my father and I weren't complaining. The wet spring had
been good for the grass. It was now tall and thick. The wooded
part of the ranch looked almost like a rain forest, and the creek
gushed like a mountain stream in Colorado after a thaw. The
windmill stood unneeded—fortunately so, because that vertical
rod (repaired years ago) was beginning to look weak again. Cattle were so fat and full they hadn't even bothered to go out looking for greener fields after high water had washed out a fence
(as we discovered a few days later) that crossed the creek. Some
of those animals might have been descendants of the puny cattle
that lived through the vicissitudes of 1953 with us, but if so they
were much more contented.

I couldn't help wondering what other differences there would
be today if this approaching cloud brought another tornado
plowing through the same area.

One notable difference would be in forecasting and in
broadcasting the prediction. The science of weather forecasting
has improved during the past quarter century, although no meteorologist can say yet exactly how a tornado is formed.† Contrib-
uting to advancement have been electronics improvements and
the use of geostationary satellites that continuously send photographs of the earth and its cloud systems from a position 22,000
miles above it. Although satellite pictures can show the eye of a
hurricane, they can't delineate a tornado. By showing cloud systems, however, the satellites help narrow the area to be watched
for possible tornadoes.

Some electronic devices newer than radar might be able to
take over from there. One piece of equipment developed re-

† In a 1975 edition of *Nature*, published in Britain, four University of California researchers offered a tongue-in-cheek speculation that today's increased number of tornadoes are caused by automobiles traveling on the
right side of the road. When they pass oncoming cars on the left, small
counterclockwise whirlwinds develop that can evolve into tornadoes.

cently is a "tornado sensor," which determines in thunderstorms the area of most intense electrical bursts as the likeliest point for tornado formation. Another development is the use of electronics equipment to measure wind speed inside thunderstorms, with the aim of predicting tornadoes.

Today the Waco office of the National Weather Service benefits (as do all others) from the satellite photographs. They are utilized first in Washington, D.C., before being transmitted with other information to various regional forecasting centers, including one for north-central Texas at the Dallas-Fort Worth Regional Airport. From regional centers a forecast is sent to offices like the one at Waco's Madison Cooper Airport, where meteorologists consider last-minute weather information and local conditions before issuing their own forecast for the immediate area. Specific tornado predictions, however, come from the Severe Storms Forecast Center, in Kansas City, which is intimately tied in with National Weather Service communications. When a possibility of tornadoes is foreseen, a local office like the one in Waco asks licensed ham radio operators throughout the area for assistance in weather watching, particularly for hail and for clouds of ominous shapes.

Another difference between today and 1953 would be in dissemination of storm information. Few citizens could remain unaware of a tornado watch (meaning the possibility of those storms has been forecast) or of a tornado warning (a no-nonsense alert, when a twister actually has been sighted nearby). Area radio and television stations would immediately broadcast the information. If these reports happened not to be heard, the wails of civil-defense sirens surely would be. They are sounded when a tornado has been sighted in the vicinity. The one that struck Waco in 1953, along with other destructive tornadoes that occurred elsewhere that same year, have been credited with proving the value of civil-defense organization for disasters other than war.

Additional warning methods have been tried. In some tornado-prone places such as Oklahoma City, television viewers leave their sets on all night. As long as the weather is calm, the picture is silent. But if a tornado threatens, a loud noise wakes up sleepers. In Oklahoma and some other states, stores are selling an alarm calculated to give warning when a tornado closes to within a mile. The device relies on a mercury switch that triggers an alarm when a connected barometer drops below twenty-nine inches of mercury.

The benefits of all this forecasting and dissemination, however, still depend on public reaction. If another tornado as deadly as that of May 11, 1953, struck the city today, casualty lists could still be as great, said Doyle Casey of the National Weather Service office in Waco (during an interview on KWTX-TV, May 11, 1976). Forecasts are more accurate and communications are improved, Casey said, but virtually everything else depends on people heeding warnings and taking precautions.

The safest place to be during a tornado seems to be entirely away from it. There are, however, some logical second choices: a storm cellar, bomb shelter, or steel-reinforced building. An engineer who examined Waco's demolished downtown section said damage would have been reduced by 90 per cent if all buildings in the tornado's path had been steel-reinforced.

Cellars in brick homes can be dangerous, because falling debris might make them death traps. Nor are automobiles safe refuges, unless they are used to outrun a tornado—preferably by traveling at right angles to it. But the worst place to be caught, generally speaking, is downtown. Buildings there prevent a good look at the advancing clouds, and street noise can mask a tornado's roar until too late. Further, deadly debris probably will fill city streets during and after a storm. But since luck plays a large part in determining where individuals get caught by tornadoes, here are some safety rules for various locations.

Downtown. Go to the lower floor of a steel-reinforced building, if possible. Or step into any building and flatten yourself against a lower-floor partition such as a wall. Always stay away from windows. If outside, lie in a depression. This might involve some split-second selecting, because heavy rain might have flooded such places as gutters.

Industrial plant. Lookouts should be posted in areas of greatest visibility to warn of a funnel cloud's approach. Then someone should shut off electrical circuits and fuel lines, if possible. Employees should be sent to buildings affording the most safety.

School. In rural areas, where a tornado's approach can be watched, the wisest action seems to be to remove children from the building, especially if it is flimsy, and have them lie flat in a ravine or other depression. In city schools having classrooms on only one side of a corridor, students should rearrange desks so that the solid sides face windows, then get under desks. If classrooms occupy both sides of a corridor, students should be taken into the hall and placed with their backs against the wall. Corridors facing south or west aren't very good choices. They tend to become "wind tunnels" in a tornado. Corridors facing north are best, those facing east next best. Upper floors and large areas such as gymnasiums should be avoided. Storerooms and closets are good shelters.

Home. A consensus of experts seems to suggest that the safest place to be is in the center of the building, on the lowest level. Other good advice is to take shelter in a small room or closet, under a stairwell, or under heavy furniture. A bathroom might be a good refuge because of the support of pipes. Stay away from chimneys. If the residence is frame and not sturdy, and if you know the tornado is approaching from the southwest, crouch in a southwest corner and hope that the wind will leave you there when it lifts the house over your head and sends it crashing in splinters somewhere. Recent research by the National Weather Service has shown, however, that the old admonition from folklore about always crouching in a southwest corner (since most tornadoes come from the southwest and would blow wreckage away from you) isn't very sound. They have found that a tornado advancing from this direction exerts greater pressure on southerly and westerly walls, which might collapse on you.

Mobile home. Get out and go somewhere else, even into a ravine or other depression. This will be inconvenient, since heavy rain and hail might accompany a tornado. Much more convenient would be a storm shelter previously provided.

Anywhere. Open some windows or doors on a side away from the approaching tornado so pressure might be equalized. Stay away from glass. Have a transistor radio available in case power for your plug-in set goes out. Afterward, wear gloves and heavy shoes while cleaning up. Watch for fallen electrical wires, broken gas pipes, and wreckage that might fall on you. Avoid smoking or lighting matches.

Safety precautions can be only as effective as the degree to which they are heeded, and people tend to be forgetful. Allen Pearson of the Severe Storms Forecast Center said (on the March 8, 1974, "Today" show) that residents of tornado-stricken areas seem to pay careful attention to weather warnings for about ten years afterward, then become smug again. His statement is supported by another storm forecaster, Robert H. Simpson, former head of the National Weather Service hurricane center in Miami, although Simpson was referring to another type of storm. "It's a very dangerous thing to go . . . long between hurricanes," he said. "It just causes a larger number of incredulous people—non-believers."

Other scientists, such as Gilbert F. White and J. Eugene Haas of the University of Colorado, have criticized the tendency of everyone from state and local officials to private citizens to ignore lessons of the past and the findings of recent research. Among their criticisms is the practice of drawing up stricter building codes to avert disasters, then failing to enforce them.

Wacoans seem not to have forgotten their lesson so quickly. Tornado forecasts are followed with careful interest by most residents—and more so than on that day many years ago. The thunderhead of May 11, 1976, did indeed spawn a funnel cloud south of the city, one that eventually vanished without touching earth, and many persons were aware of it. That's a difference that time has made.

Still another is in the look of the city, although ugly spots remain. Unfortunately, some of them are near the heavily used Highway I-35, linking Canada with Mexico, and are easily noticed by thousands of tourists every week. Off the highway, however, are other scenes. A downtown mall, where strollers can walk along a section of Austin Avenue barred to traffic—the same street where, in 1953, debris buried automobiles and killed people. A marina and countless other improvements on the

Brazos River, which has been dammed to make a lake along a strip fronting the city. An excursion boat named the *Brazos Queen*. New construction and vast landscaping on the Baylor University campus, which has expanded and replaced a large shantytown. An urban renewal program that has eliminated other run-down sections and has provided better living conditions for people who once resided there. The city's post-tornado success may be summarized by the presentation to Waco, on June 11, 1976, of the Governor's Community Achievement Award for beautification. It was a result of work begun years ago, soon after the 1953 disaster.

Beatrice Ramirez spoke of another result. After emerging alive from the wreckage of the Dennis Building and after recovering from her injuries, she was given a new job. *Tribune-Herald* editor Sam Wood read her account of experiences submitted for publication in his newspaper and was so impressed with her detail and drama that he hired her as a reporter.

On the first anniversary of the tornado, she took a personal inventory and decided that "[it] makes you feel just as new as the beautiful buildings that have come up since the storm . . . [and] with the new look, a new feeling, and a complete new life. . . . Thank you, God."

I believe that for Beatrice Ramirez and for thousands of others, the tragedy resulted in triumph. The tornado of May 11, 1953, eliminated countless dreams, but it is a tribute to the human spirit that new dreams usually emerge from the ruins of old ones.

Acknowledgments and Bibliography

This narrative has been based not only on publications and other sources listed below but on my own recollections and notes of that time and on my father's and mother's memories of May 11, 1953, given before their deaths.

Eyewitness accounts of Waco tornado survivors are based mostly on information given immediately afterward, when many details were still vivid. There are a few exceptions to this that are obvious in the text. Many of the accounts utilized were written immediately afterward, by survivors themselves, for the Waco *Tribune-Herald*. My appreciation goes to Woody M. Barron, managing editor, for permission to use them. Most of these accounts involve other individuals in addition to the eyewitnesses, but the source of information is, I believe, evident in the text.

This is meant to be representative of the whole. Other persons not mentioned herein might have been able to tell stories equally or more dramatic, but the research had to end somewhere. Completeness would have meant including thousands of names and would have resulted in a book too large to publish.

Names, ages, and titles in the Waco tornado section are in accord with 1953 usage. Numerous persons referred to have died.

Others have remarried. Most have different jobs, or are retired. None of this is considered here.

No dialogue has been invented. All direct quotations have been used as found in research. Some spellings have been changed for consistency. It was the "Joy Theatre," by name, but I have used "Joy Theater" to be consistent with the spelling of the latter word elsewhere in the text. For consistency, I have also eliminated all accent marks in names of Mexican-Americans. Some persons concerned prefer their usage, but others do not.

Various newspaper files also were used. Because of the speed with which newspapers are printed, I have sought to verify accuracy of stories (as, for instance, checking spellings of names and addresses against the 1953 City Directory). In my opinion, the best and most accurate reporting of the 1953 tornado was done by the Waco *Tribune-Herald*, under very difficult conditions. I have used information that appeared there, and in that regard I acknowledge assistance from numerous reporters and editors. Some of them I knew personally; some I didn't; several are deceased. Their names:

John Banta, Woody Barron, Dave Campbell, Reba Campbell, Tom Caulfield, Betty Dollins, Earl Golding, Oscar Larnce, Jules Loh, Leo Lyons, Murray Neal, Harry Provence, George Raborn, Jinx Tucker, Clarence Weikel, Chris Whitcraft and Sam Wood.

Three *Tribune-Herald* stories that appeared recently have proved informative, too. They are these:

"Professional Forecasters Find No 'Normal' Weather," by Jack Flanders, June 1, 1974; "Schools Ready Twister Defenses," by Bruce Westbrook, May 4, 1974; "Weather Bureau 'Local' Agency," by Ron Wilson, December 22, 1975.

Tornado accounts by some out-of-town newsmen proved helpful. These journalists included:

Paul Crume, Dallas *Morning News;* Larry Ingram, Temple *Daily Telegram* (the managing editor who called me May 11, 1953, with the request to go to Hewitt); Wilbur Martin, Associated Press; Fred A. McCabe, United Press (as it was known then); Woody Montgomery, Temple *Daily Telegram;* Sarah McClendon, Washington correspondent for the Temple *Daily Telegram* (and other newspapers); and Tommy Turner, Dallas

Morning News (who did an excellent job of coverage for his newspaper after he learned that a tornado had indeed struck).

My appreciation also goes to staff members of the Barker Texas History Center of the University of Texas, the Baylor University Library, the McLennan Community College Library, the Newspaper Collection of the University of Texas, the Texas State Library, the University of Texas Archives (especially for the Harry Estill Moore Papers), and the University of Texas Library.

Picture credits are as follows:

Cirrus clouds. Author's collection; photograph by author.

Mammatocumulus. Author's collection, from *Spotter's Guide for Identifying and Reporting Severe Local Storms* (see bibliography).

Squall line clouds. Author's collection, from *Spotter's Guide*.

Distant thunderstorm. Author's collection, from *Spotter's Guide*.

Developing funnel. Author's collection, from *Spotter's Guide*.

Tornado. Author's collection, from *Spotter's Guide*.

1919 Nebraska tornado. This photograph of a tornado near Elmwood, Nebraska, April 6, 1919, was made by W. A. Wood. It has appeared in several publications, including *Why the Weather?* (see the bibliography).

1884 South Dakota tornado. Probably the oldest (and certainly one of the oldest) photographs of a tornado ever made, this picture (by F. W. Robinson) has been widely reproduced, from files of the U. S. Weather Bureau (now National Weather Service).

Waco damage. Photograph by Jimmie Willis, Waco.

Franklin Avenue, Waco. Photograph by Jimmie Willis.

City, county map showing damage area. Adapted by the author from a map in *Waco Disaster Operation* (see the bibliography), provided by Wiley Stem, 1953 national-guard commander.

Cleaning up wreckage. Photograph by Waco *Tribune-Herald*.

Days later. Photograph by Waco *Tribune-Herald*.

Austin Avenue today, the Mall. Author's collection; photograph by author.

Brazos River, city in distance. Author's collection; photograph by author.

The *Brazos Queen*. Author's collection; photograph by author.

Author, father, ranch windmill, 1976. Author's collection; photograph by Janet Weems, July 4, 1976.

Following is a bibliography of source material.

BOOKS

Meteorology

Albright, John Grover. *Physical Meteorology*. New York: Prentice-Hall, 1939.

Bathurst, G. B. "The Earliest Recorded Tornado," *Weather*, Vol. 19. London: Royal Meteorological Society, 1964.

Battan, Louis J. *The Nature of Violent Storms*. Garden City, N.Y.: Anchor Books, 1961.

Bonacina, L. C. W. "The Widecombe Calamity of 1638," *Weather*, Vol. 1. London: Royal Meteorological Society, 1946.

Brooks, Charles Franklin. *Why the Weather?* New York: Harcourt, Brace, 1924.

Byers, Horace Robert. *General Meteorology*. New York: McGraw-Hill, 1959.

Cline, Isaac Monroe. *Storms, Floods and Sunshine*. New Orleans: Pelican, 1945.

Cline, Joseph L. *When the Heavens Frowned*. Dallas: Mathis, Van Nort, 1946. (J. L. Cline was Isaac Cline's brother.)

Critchfield, Howard J. *General Climatology*. Englewood Cliffs, N.J.: Prentice-Hall, 1960.

Dunn, Gordon E.; and Miller, Banner I. *Atlantic Hurricanes*. Baton Rouge: L.S.U. Press, 1960.

Encyclopedia Americana, Vols. 18, 29. New York: Americana Corporation, 1954. (This edition, although old, still has a good discussion of the history of meteorology and the history of what was once called the U. S. Weather Bureau. It was used for both.)

Finley, J. P. *Report on the Character of Six Hundred Tornadoes*. Washington, D.C.: U. S. War Department, Signal Office, 1884.

———. *Report on the Tornadoes of May 29 and 30, 1879*. Washington, D.C.: Government Printing Office, 1881.

Flohn, Hermann. *Climate and Weather*. New York: World University Library, 1969.

Flora, Snowden D. *Tornadoes of the United States*. Norman: University of Oklahoma Press, 1954.

Freeman, John C. "Radar Echoes in Tornado Situations," *Proceedings of the Conference on Radio Meteorology* [November 9–12, 1953]. Austin: University of Texas Bureau of Engineering Research, 1954.

Humphreys, W. J. *Weather Proverbs and Paradoxes*. Baltimore: Williams & Wilkins, 1923.

Lane, Frank W. *The Elements Rage*. Philadelphia: Chilton, 1965.

Lehr, Paul E.; Burnett, R. Will; and Zim, Herbert S. *Weather*. New York: Golden Press, 1965. (One of the best weather books for children this author has seen. It will also serve adults possessing little technical background. Good illustrations, by Harry McNaught.)

Meek, J. B. "Account of a Tornado which occurred in Spruce Creek Valley, Centre County, Pennsylvania," *Annual Report . . . of the Smithsonian Institution, 1871*. Washington, D.C.: Government Printing Office, 1873.

National Audubon Society. *The Audubon Nature Encyclopedia*, Vol. 11. Philadelphia: Curtis, 1965. (Has a good discussion of weather for young readers.)

Ross, Frank, Jr. *Storms and Man*. New York: Lothrop, Lee & Shepard, 1971.

Spotter's Guide for Identifying and Reporting Severe Local Storms. Washington, D.C.: U. S. Department of Commerce, National Oceanic and Atmospheric Administration, 1973.

Stinson, J. Robert. *The Waco Tornado of May 11, 1953*. St. Louis: St. Louis University Institute of Technology Report No. 6 [n.d.]. (Obtained on interlibrary loan at McLennan Community College, Waco, from the Atmospheric Sciences Library, National Oceanic and Atmospheric Administration. My appreciation to both libraries.)

Sutton, Oliver G. *The Challenge of the Atmosphere*. New York: Harper & Row, 1961.

Tannehill, I. R. *Hurricanes: Their Nature and History*. Princeton, N.J.: Princeton University Press, 1954.

Trewartha, Glenn T. *The Earth's Problem Climates*. Madison: University of Wisconsin Press, 1961.

U. S. Navy. *The Bluejackets' Manual*. Annapolis: U. S. Naval Institute, 1946. (My old copy, but still current and clear in its brief section on weather.)

Other Aspects of Weather

Brown, Billye Walker; and Brown, Walter R. *Historical Catastrophes: Hurricanes and Tornadoes.* Reading, Mass.: Addison-Wesley, 1972.

Delury, George E. (editor). *The World Almanac and Book of Facts, 1976.* New York: Newspaper Enterprise Association, 1975.

Forbis, William H. *The Cowboys.* New York: Time-Life Books, 1973.

Frazier, James George. *The Golden Bough,* Vol. 1. New York: Macmillan, 1935.

Freuchen, Peter; with Loth, David. *Peter Freuchen's Book of the Seven Seas.* New York: Julian Messner, 1957.

Georgakas, Dan. *Red Shadows.* New York: Doubleday, 1973.

In Time of Emergency: a Citizen's Handbook on Nuclear Attack, Natural Disasters. Washington, D.C.: Department of Defense, Office of Civil Defense, 1968.

Kirk, Ruth. *Desert: the American Southwest.* Boston: Houghton Mifflin, 1973.

Laffon, Polk. *Tornado.* New York: Harper & Row, 1975.

Mails, Thomas E. *The People Called Apache.* Englewood Cliffs, N.J.: Prentice-Hall, 1974.

Oxford English Dictionary, Vol. 11. London: Clarendon Press, 1961.

Stefansson, Vilhjalmur. *The Friendly Arctic.* New York: Macmillan, 1921.

Tuffy, Barbara. *1001 Questions Answered About Storms and Other Natural Air Disasters.* New York: Dodd, Mead, 1970.

Webb, Walter Prescott. *The Great Plains.* Boston: Ginn, 1931.

Weems, John Edward. *A Weekend in September.* New York: Henry Holt, 1957. (Non-fiction account of the 1900 Galveston hurricane.)

Wells, H. G. *The Outline of History.* Garden City, N.Y.: Garden City Books, 1949.

Local Information

Carver, Charles. *Brann and the Iconoclast.* Austin: University of Texas Press, 1957.

Conger, Roger N. *A Pictorial History of Waco with a Reprint of Highlights of Waco History.* Waco: Texian Press, 1964.

Kelley, Dayton (editor). *The Handbook of Waco and McLennan County, Texas.* Waco: Texian Press, 1972.

Lynch, Dudley. *Tornado: Texas Demon in the Wind.* Waco: Texian Press, 1970.

Manchester, William. *The Glory and the Dream.* Boston: Little, Brown, 1973.

Moore, Harry Estill. *Tornadoes over Texas: a Study of Waco and San Angelo in Disaster.* Austin: University of Texas Press, 1958. (Sociological examination of the tragedies.)

Moore, Walter B.; and Pass, Fred R. *Texas Almanac and State Industrial Guide, 1974–1975.* Dallas: A. H. Belo, 1973.

Preliminary Report: Waco-San Angelo Disaster Study. Austin: University of Texas Department of Sociology, 1954.

Smith, J. W. "Which Way Waco?" *Baylor Business Studies, No. 11.* Waco: Baylor University School of Business, June 1952.

Texas National Guard. *Waco Disaster Operation.* [n.p, n.d.]

Waco Disaster, May 11, 1953. Dallas (regional office): Federal Civil Defense Administration, 1953.

Waco (McLennan County, Tex.) City Directory, Vol. 37. Dallas: Morrison & Fourmy, 1953.

Waco-San Angelo Disaster Study: Report of Second Year's Work. Austin: University of Texas Department of Sociology, 1955.

Webb, Walter Prescott (editor). *The Handbook of Texas,* Vols. 1–2. Austin: Texas State Historical Association, 1952.

MAGAZINES

Meteorology

Battan, Louis J. "Killers from the Clouds," *Natural History,* April 1975.

Keller, Will. [Tornado story prepared by Justice, A. A.]. *Monthly Weather Review,* May 1930.

"The Press Reports the Natchez Tornado—7 May, 1840." *Weatherwise,* April 1966.

"What's Wrong with the Weather?" *U. S. News & World Report,* June 26, 1953. (Interview with head of the Weather Bureau, Francis W. Reichelderfer.)

Whitaker, H. R. "Everything You Always Wanted to Know About Tornadoes," *Science Digest,* April 1975.

Winston, Jay S. "The Weather and Circulation of May 1953," *Monthly Weather Review,* May 1953.

Other Aspects of Weather

"Bombs over the U. S." *Time*, March 1, 1976.

Irwin, T. K. "Weather and You: Your Illnesses, Your Moods in Rain or Shine," *Family Weekly*, September 14, 1975. (Includes interview with Dr. Helmut E. Landsberg)

Local Information

Baden, Ira J.; as told to Parham, Robert H. "My 45 Seconds Inside the Tornado," *The Saturday Evening Post*, July 11, 1953. (Used by permission of *The Saturday Evening Post*)

"Block at a Time," *Business Week*, May 23, 1953.

Dominis, John (photographer). "Search for Miss Matkin," *Life*, May 25, 1953.

"It Can Happen Almost Anywhere," *The American City*, July 1953.

"Swirling Death," *Newsweek*, May 25, 1953.

NEWSPAPERS

Meteorology

Associated Press. Story on Connecticut Weather Control Board, datelined Hartford, appeared in various newspapers of July 5, 1975.

McElheny, Victor K. "How Killer Tornadoes Were Formed," New York *Times*, April 5, 1974.

Sullivan, Walter. "4 Researchers Link U. S. Tornadoes to Driving on Right Side of the Road," New York *Times*, January 25, 1975.

United Press International. Story on skyscrapers changing rainfall pattern, datelined Houston, appeared in various newspapers of May 6, 1974.

Other Aspects of Weather

Associated Press. Story on Roy Bennett and the tornado, datelined Wichita Falls, Texas, appeared in various newspapers of April 3, 1966.

——. Story on new ideas for protection in tornadoes, datelined Washington, appeared April 7, 1974.

——. Story with remarks by Gilbert F. White and J. Eugene Haas, datelined Washington, appeared June 17, 1975.

——. Story on disarmament discussion, datelined Geneva, appeared August 28, 1975.

——. Story quoting Henry Lansford about the American Great Plains, datelined Washington, appeared November 16, 1975.

——. Story quoting Erik Eckholm on desert encroachment, datelined Boston, appeared February 20, 1976.

Chicago Daily News Syndicate. Story (by Donald Zochert) on man's being a volcano appeared April 14, 1974.

Drumright (Oklahoma) *Journal,* July 25, 1974.

Tulsa (Oklahoma) *Sunday World,* March 23, 1975.

United Press International. Story about tornado alarm, datelined Lubbock, Texas, appeared February 25, 1974.

——. Story about house insulation, datelined Cookeville, Tennessee, appeared April 5, 1974.

——. Story about meteorologists testing new tornado sensor, datelined Oklahoma City, appeared April 7, 1974.

——. Story about improved tornado warnings, datelined Houston, appeared April 9, 1974.

——. Story about 1974 tornado in Gorki, datelined Moscow, appeared July 5, 1974.

——. Story about "flying boats" on Lake Pepin, no dateline, appeared August 22, 1975.

——. Story about weather satellite in orbit, datelined Cape Canaveral, appeared October 18, 1975.

——. Story about winter storm deaths, datelined Houston, appeared February 18, 1976.

——. Story about the woman, the van, and the corn field, no dateline (but it was "west of Ogden, Illinois"), appeared March 21, 1976.

——. Story with interview of Robert H. Simpson, datelined Corpus Christi, appeared June 7, 1976.

Local Information

Associated Press. Story about Mrs. Carbajal appeared May 14, 1953.

Austin *American-Statesman,* May 12, 1953. (For tornado stories)

Dallas *Morning News,* May 6–18, 1953. (For weather maps and tornado stories)

Dallas *Times-Herald,* May 12, 1953. (For tornado stories)

Forth Worth *Star-Telegram,* May 12, 1953. (For tornado stories)

Houston *Chronicle,* May 12, 1953. (For tornado stories)

Houston *Post,* May 12, 1953. (For tornado stories)

San Angelo (Texas) *Standard-Times,* May 12, 1953. (For tornado stories)

———, May 10, 1970. (For tornado stories)

San Antonio *Express,* May 12, 1953. (For tornado stories)

San Antonio *Light,* May 12, 1953. (For tornado stories)

Temple (Texas) *Daily Telegram,* May 11–13, 1953. (For tornado stories)

United Press (as it was then named). Story on Mrs. Coates and Sandy waiting at home, by Fred A. McCabe, appeared May 14, 1953.

Waco *News Tribune,* Waco *Times Herald,* and Waco *Tribune-Herald* (morning, afternoon, and Sunday newspapers owned by the same company) files of April, May, and June 1953; and files of anniversary editions (of the May 11, 1953, tornado) through 1976. Newspapers of May 11–21, 1953, were bound and entitled *Waco Tornado;* a set is in the Waco Public Library.

TELEVISION AND RADIO PROGRAMS

NBC News Special. Xenia, Ohio, tornado. Narrated by Floyd Kalber. Autumn, 1974.

Region Ten News. Doyle Casey interview, KWTX-TV, Waco. May 11, 1976.

NBC "Today" show. Allen Pearson interview. March 8, 1974.

OTHER SOURCES

Personal interviews, Correspondence, Other Assistance

Candace E. Adams, University of Texas Press, Austin; C. A. Anderson, U. S. Weather Bureau, Waco (meteorologist, now deceased, interviewed in 1956); John Banta, *Tribune-Herald,* Waco; Woody Barron, *Tribune-Herald,* Waco; Walter Bradbury, Cindy Harman, Kathy Heavey, and Frank Hoffman, Doubleday, New York; Carl Brandt, Brandt & Brandt, New York; Dave Campbell, *Tribune-Herald,* Waco; John Freeman, Institute for Storm Research, University of St. Thomas, Houston; Joseph Galway, National Severe Storms Forecast Center, Kansas City; William S. Gardiner, *The Saturday Evening Post,* Indianapolis, Indiana; Lourdes I. Maier, Institute for Storm Research, University of St. Thomas, Houston; Andrew Oerke,

Washington, D.C.; Allen Pearson, National Severe Storms Forecast Center, Kansas City; Mrs. Pearl Pruitt, Ponca City, Oklahoma; Jones Ramsey, Austin, Texas; Helena P. Schmitt, Atmospheric Sciences Library, National Oceanic and Atmospheric Administration, Silver Spring, Maryland; Barbara Spielman, University of Texas Press, Austin; Mr. and Mrs. Wiley Stem, Waco; Tommy Turner, Waco; Donald Weems, Austin; Jane Weems, Waco; Janet Weems, Waco; Jimmie Willis, Waco; and Juanita Willis, Waco.

The list of tornado dead published in the Waco *News Tribune* and the Waco *Times Herald* of May 16, 1953, included these names and addresses. All are city residents unless otherwise identified.

Melad Abraham, Route 4, Box 707; Jack Downman Adams, 2217 Pine; Raymond C. Anderson, James Street.

Mildred Jean Bailey, Lott, Texas; Cecil Berry, 1228 Maxfield; Edward Berry, 115 Karem; Rush Berry, 3528 Austin; Billy Betros, 1204 South Twenty-second; Bertha Blume, New Robinson Road; Robert William Boerner, 2525 Austin; Beveridge C. Boyd, 1623 Colcord; Cynthia Britt, no address; Edward M. Britt, South Tenth; Foy Brown, 1712 Park Avenue; Mrs. George Brown, Robinson Road; Cecil Walter Buhl, 1003 North Thirteenth; Thomas Busby, Temple, Texas; John W. Byrd, 1305 Gurley.

Marie Jones Carter, Palestine, Texas; Jerry Davis Childress, South Eighth; J. W. Coates, 3904 Maple; Elijah Coffelt, 423 North Twenty-third; Opal Colley, 505 North Twelfth; Ray Laurence Comer, Route 10, Box 400; Esteven Perez Cortez, 401 North Second; Bertha Cotton, 110 Webster; Tom Courtney, 927 South Second.

Clee Degrate, South Tenth; William James Dobrovolney, 2400 Lasker; Mrs. Autie Mae Duncan, 2704 Lasker.

C. J. Eschenberg, 625 Rose (added later as 114th victim).

David Franklin Farquhar, 1524 North Thirteenth.

Irving Ginsburg, 2316 Proctor; Minnie Ola Graves, 2017 Park.

W. V. Hardin, 217 South Third; Earl Harris, Hatton Street; Sam Haynes, Route 4, Box 794; Steve Heath, South Third; Archie Henderson, no address; Willis Hightower, no address; Edward T. Hoare, 912 South Twenty-eighth; Susie Hoare, 912 South Twenty-eighth; Sam Horne, Bridge Street; Tom Hurst, 906 North Thirteenth.

Helen James, 3724 North Twentieth; Keith James, 3724 North Twentieth; Virginia Lee Jenkins, 210 Warren; Barbara Johnson, 4001 Austin; Ruby Lee Jones, Ridge Street.

Johnny B. King, Earl Avenue; Mrs. W. A. Kunze, Lott, Texas.

Edward Lewis, Anson, Texas; Ola Lloyd, 2902 Lasker; William Henry Lytle, 2915 Windsor.

Billy Mahares, YMCA; Harry M. Mahoney, Dallas, Texas; Ollie Mann, 2000 Ethel; Irene Reed Matthews, no address; Gussie Mayfield, 1510 Windsor; Vera McCarver, 2708 Connor; Albert McCrary, James Connally Air Force Base; Jim McCuin, 618 Indiana; Eugene Mendoza, North Fourth; Joyce Marie Miers, North Twelfth; Lonie James Motten, East Clay; Charles B. Mullen, Earle Hotel.

J. P. Neal, Jr., Route 8, Box 50; Joe C. Neely, 2737 Herring; Mrs. Joe C. Neely, 2737 Herring; Frances Nemmer, Route 10; Garfield Nemmer, Route 10.

George Pappas, 625 Maryland; Charlie Parker, 515 Clifton; Cecil Marion Parten, Lott, Texas; Earl Pattillo, 3210 Morrow; Bobbie Jean Peoples, Route 8; Dennis Peoples, Route 8; Clarence Potter, 113 South Fourth; Vernon Powell, 429 East Walnut; Vada Prather, 2106 South Ninth.

Christine Casarez Romo, 919 South First; Willie James Roquemore, 601 Carver; Arthur Lee Ross, 505 Carver; George Conrad Roth, North Twelfth; Raymond S. Ruiz, 2700 Cleveland.

Danny Sanchez, 401 South Twelfth; E. A. Sermas, 420 Austin; Victor A. Sermas, 420 Austin; Roger K. Sharbutt, Bellmead, Texas; Hal E. Shelton, 1116 Morrow; Eugene Cooper Sherrod, Route 1; Guy Sims, Route 7, Box 242; Stan Skyles, 3800 Gorman; Joe Smith, no address; Lillian Smith, 15 Pump Station Alley; Dave Spero, 726 North Tenth; Vernon D. Starks, 1801 South Nineteenth; Betty Lou Stewart, Lott, Texas; W. R. Stewart, 1014 Speight.

Annie Mae Taylor, 311 Speight; Billy Vernon Taylor, 1611 North Twenty-first; Mabel Thaxton, 1704 Columbus; Lloyd Torres, 1520 Webster; Knox Todd, 712 North Eighth; Luther Tristan, 108 Webster; Mrs. S. B. Turner, 1912 Connor.

Jerry Utley, 2425 Sanger.

Walter Van Hook, Harrison Street; Felix Villareal, 205 Bosque.

Sammie Ray Warren, 1200 Lexington; William Frank Watkins, 3032 Bosque; Edward Homer Wiley, 2122 Homan; Arthur Woodson, no address.

Lou Younes, 1670 North Seventeenth.

The total of 114 is disputed. Some say other deaths should be added. One man mentioned is C. J. Ott, a store manager who worked throughout Monday night helping to clean debris and died of a heart attack early Tuesday morning.

INDEX

S